MediaWiki Skins Design

Designing attractive skins and templates for your MediaWiki site

Richard Carter

PUBLISHING

BIRMINGHAM - MUMBAI

MediaWiki Skins Design

First published: August 2008

Production Reference: 1140808

Published by Packt Publishing Ltd.
32 Lincoln Road
Olton
Birmingham, B27 6PA, UK.

ISBN 978-1-847195-20-3

www.packtpub.com

Cover Image by Nilesh Mohite (nilpreet2000@yahoo.co.in)

Credits

Author

Richard Carter

Reviewer

Peter De Decker

Senior Acquisition Editor

David Barnes

Development Editor

Swapna V. Verlekar

Technical Editor

Shilpa Dube

Copy Editor

Sneha Kulkarni

Editorial Team Leaders

Mithil Kulkarni

Akshara Aware

Project Manager

Abhijeet Deobhakta

Project Coordinator

Lata Basantani

Indexer

Rekha Nair

Proofreader

Dirk Manuel

Production Coordinator

Aparna Bhagat

Cover Work

Aparna Bhagat

About the Author

Richard Carter started as a freelance web designer in Leicestershire, UK, before moving to the North-East to study at Durham University, where he met his business partner. He is now Senior Partner of Peacock Carter (http://www.peacockcarter. co.uk), a Newcastle-based creative partnership offering website design and corporate identity development to small, medium, and large businesses in UK and further afield.

Richard's interests include tea-drinking, swimming, and periodically reorganizing the office furniture. He now lives in Durham, slightly too close to the Cathedral's bells.

Contact: richard.carter@peacockcarter.co.uk

Firstly, I'd like to thank David Barnes of Packt for helping to nurture the idea for this book, and to those behind the scenes at Packt - particularly Lata - for their help guiding me through their processes.

Michael, my business partner, is owed thanks too, for keeping the business running during those times I needed to concentrate on the book, as are Danni, my friends, and my family, all of whom were supportive throughout (and probably relieved that I had something to do with my time other than creating websites).

Additional thanks are due to Peter, the reviewer, who had plenty of useful and interesting suggestions for the book.

About the Reviewer

Peter De Decker is the author of a MediaWiki extension called IpbWiki which is an integration plugin that integrates the forum software Invision Power Board with the Mediawiki engine with the main purpose of giving the applications a unified look and login. During the ongoing creation of this extension he has become an expert in understanding the MediaWiki source code and layout.

As Peter had previously reviewed the MediaWiki Administrator book it was only logical to also use his MediaWiki expertise for this book on MediaWiki skinning.

During his day job Peter works as a Database Adminstrator for SQL Server in a company called Financial Architects, where he is part of the Core Development team. His main task there is to provide a solid product base which the other teams in the firm can use or expand up on. As a secondary profession, he sells software and services through his company called Global Soft. When he's not working he likes to exercise his hobbies: running, biking, collecting comics, and playing snooker.

Contact: `ipbwiki@gmail.com`

Alternative Email: `peterdedecker@gmail.com`

I'd like to thank Richard Carter for writing this book on skinning MediaWiki and hope that it will help to further spread the love for this wonderful wiki engine.

Table of Contents

Preface

MediaWiki Skins Design takes you through the process of creating a new skin (design) for your wiki, from thinking about your wiki's audience and purpose, to adding social media features, and even styling the wiki for printing.

What This Book Covers

Chapter 1 takes a look at existing wikis on the web, and introduces the case study used throughout the book.

Chapter 2 goes through setting your new skin as the wiki's default skin, and styling the different views of the wiki's primary content that will be seen by your wiki's visitors.

Chapter 3 describes how the interface elements such as the navigation links and search feature can be styled, as well as how to customize the edit toolbar.

Chapter 4 takes a look at the <head> attributes in MediaWiki, and begins to structure the case study wiki in to a newer, more suitable layout.

Chapter 5 covers more in-depth PHP and MediaWiki functions you can use to enhance your new MediaWiki skin.

Chapter 6 describes how to design and create a visual hierarchy for your wiki's content.

Chapter 7 describes useful JavaScript code and CSS that you can use to enhance your wiki and its features.

Chapter 8 explains how to integrate your wiki with social networking sites, and how to use services such as YouTube and Twitter on your MediaWiki.

Chapter 9 takes a look at deploying your new MediaWiki skin, and the options you have when licensing your wiki's skin for others to use.

Chapter 10 explains how to style your wiki's content for printing.

In *Appendix A*, the different modes of interpretation such as Standards mode and Quirks mode are discussed.

What You Need for This Book

Access to a server, either available on your computer locally, or on the web, is useful to test your skin. Additionally, you will need to have installed MediaWiki, and have full permissions to edit the files associated with it. Other than this, a simple text editor or any HTML/CSS/PHP editor with syntax highlighting will be required.

Who is This Book For

This book is aimed at web designers or wiki administrators who want to customize the look of MediaWiki by using custom skins.

You will already have a MediaWiki installation that you are targeting with your skin. This might be your own installation, or you might be a designer developing a custom look for a client. The book does not cover setting up or using MediaWiki, except for features specifically related to skinning.

This book assumes that you are familiar with CSS and HTML, but no prior knowledge of PHP is required.

Conventions

In this book, you will find a number of styles of text that distinguish between different kinds of information. Here are some examples of these styles, and an explanation of their meaning.

Code words in the text are shown as follows: "We can include other contexts through the use of the `include` directive."

A block of code is shown as follows:

```
<link rel="shortcut icon" href="/favicon.ico" />
<link rel="search" type="application/opensearchdescription+xml"
href="/richard.carter/book/v1/opensearch_desc.php" title="JazzMeet
(English)" />
```

When we wish to draw your attention to a particular part of a code block, the relevant lines or items will be bold:

```
<style type="text/css">
<?php $this->html('usercss'   ) ?>
</style>
```

New terms and **important words** are introduced in a bold-type font. Words that you see on the screen, in menus or dialog boxes for example, appear in the text like this: "Select the **Skins** tab and you will find your new skin is in the list of skins that are available on your wiki".

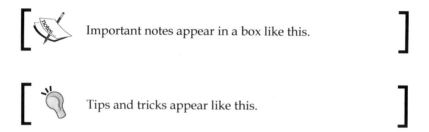

Important notes appear in a box like this.

Tips and tricks appear like this.

Reader Feedback

Feedback from our readers is always welcome. Let us know what you think about this book, what you liked or may have disliked. Reader feedback is important for us to develop titles that you really get the most out of.

To send us general feedback, simply drop an email to feedback@packtpub.com, making sure to mention the book title in the subject of your message.

If there is a book that you need and would like to see us publish, please send us a note in the **SUGGEST A TITLE** form on www.packtpub.com or email suggest@packtpub.com.

If there is a topic that you have expertise in and you are interested in either writing or contributing to a book, see our author guide on www.packtpub.com/authors.

Customer Support

Now that you are the proud owner of a Packt book, we have a number of things to help you to get the most from your purchase.

Downloading the Example Code for the Book

Visit `http://www.packtpub.com/files/code/5203_Code.zip` to directly download the example code.

The downloadable files contain instructions on how to use them.

Errata

Although we have taken every care to ensure the accuracy of our contents, mistakes do happen. If you find a mistake in one of our books—maybe a mistake in text or code—we would be grateful if you would report this to us. By doing this you can save other readers from frustration, and help to improve subsequent versions of this book. If you find any errata, report them by visiting `http://www.packtpub.com/support`, selecting your book, clicking on the **let us know** link, and entering the details of your errata. Once your errata are verified, your submission will be accepted and the errata added to the list of existing errata (if any). Existing errata can be viewed by selecting your title from `http://www.packtpub.com/support`.

Piracy

Piracy of copyright material on the Internet is an ongoing problem across all media. At Packt, we take the protection of our copyright and licenses very seriously. If you come across any illegal copies of our works in any form on the Internet, please provide the location address or website name immediately so we can pursue a remedy.

Please contact us at `copyright@packtpub.com` with a link to the suspected pirated material.

We appreciate your help in protecting our authors, and our ability to bring you valuable content.

Questions

You can contact us at `questions@packtpub.com` if you are having a problem with some aspect of the book, and we will do our best to address it.

1
Introduction

For some websites, wikis along with blogs (weblogs) have become an essential component in order to collaborate in online editing. MediaWiki is one of the most popular wikis in use, with features such as integration of YouTube videos. It also has plugins that allow forums such as Invision Power Board to integrate with MediaWiki.

By playing around with MediaWiki's PHP template files and Cascading Style Sheets (CSS), almost any design can be recreated in MediaWiki. The more complicated the design is, the more work will be involved in skinning MediaWiki to match it!

In this chapter, we will discuss the following:

- The importance of skinning your wiki
- The MediaWiki skins supplied with the MediaWiki install
- Some examples of creative MediaWiki skins in action
- A case study, which will be the focus of the techniques we discuss throughout the book.

For the purpose of this book, you should install MediaWiki and complete the basic configuration (refer to `http://www.installationwiki.org`). Then begin restyling your wiki. A basic working knowledge of eXtensible Hyper Text Markup Language (XHTML) and Cascading Style Sheets (CSS) is required. An understanding of PHP as well as MediaWiki (for example, being able to edit pages) will be a bonus.

Examples of MediaWiki Skins

There is little variation in the MediaWiki skins of each wiki, when we take their popularity into consideration. A few examples of existing wikis will give you an idea of what can be achieved. In particular, we will look at Wikipedia, which has become synonymous with wikis, AboutUs, and the WordPress Codex.

Wikipedia: The Monotony of MonoBook

Wikipedia, the "free encyclopedia that everyone can edit", is the most well-known example of a MediaWiki implementation. Wikipedia uses a slightly modified version of the "MonoBook" theme, the default MediaWiki skin that is supplied with the installation.

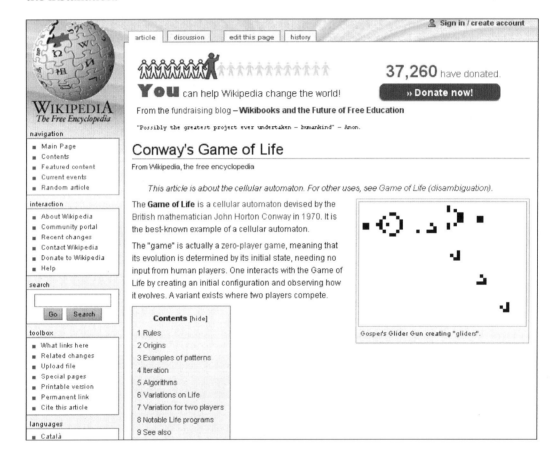

It is surprising that only a few webmasters redesign their wiki— the 'MonoBook' theme supplied with MediaWiki's installation and used on Wikipedia, is a very common sight on wikis. The logo is often the only element that is changed in the design. The problem with MonoBook is that Wikipedia has become so popular that the MonoBook theme is usually associated with Wikipedia rather than MediaWiki. Although a great change in the overall layout of components can cause visitors to the wiki to become disorientated, a reasonable amount of change can be made before this occurs, so this should not deter us too much.

MediaWiki comes with a selection of six themes: "Chick", "Classic", "Cologne Blue", "MonoBook", "Nostalgia", and "Simple". Another theme, "MySkin", allows you to specify the stylesheet to be used by creating a valid CSS file at User:YourUserName/myskin.css in your wiki's namespace. Apart from the "MonoBook" skin, the other MediaWiki themes are not used very frequently. This is because aesthetically, they are not very appealing.

As an online encyclopedia, Wikipedia's skin is under-stated. A too bright design would hinder the visitors' focus not only from the web page content, but also the most important aspects of the website. Let's face it: MonoBook is an ugly skin. It is grey, dull, and unappealing to new visitors. Wikipedia's saving grace is its content; but the supposed focus of each page's primarily monochrome content is lost to the plethora of blue links surrounding the content.

The use of a small font allows a lot of content to be displayed on the screen, and is ideal for an encyclopedia with long articles. But the amount of content on the screen makes it hard to read for a long period of time.

There is too much information on the screen, such as links to that versions of the page in different languages and log in and register links. Because of this, no single element on the page really stands out. This means the search box is unlikely to be used unless you are a frequent visitor to Wikipedia, and only those "in the know" will be aware of the ability to edit pages.

Bog Standard

MediaWiki's Standard skin is another one that is supplied with the installation.

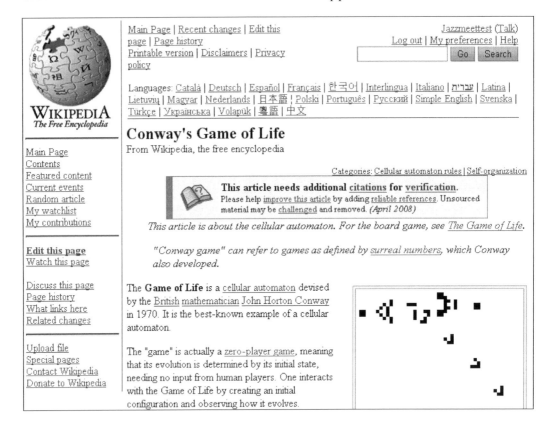

Not surprisingly, there is nothing special about this skin. It displays the content in a plain, featureless way, which may be suitable for Wikipedia, but will not help you to differentiate your wiki from other wikis.

In Standard, the navigation, including the links to the page in different languages is split between the left-hand column and the top of the screen. This unnecessarily pushes the page's primary content even further down the page.

Nostalgia

Nostalgia is similar to MediaWiki's Standard skin. It is similar to Standard in placing various (probably infrequently used) links above the page's primary content. Unlike Standard, the Nostalgia skin aligns the wiki's logo to the right rather than the left, making it less of a focus on the page.

Conway's Game of Life

From Wikipedia, the free encyclopedia

Main Page | Recent changes | Edit this page | Page history | Log out |

Special pages [ ] Go

Printable version | Disclaimers | Privacy policy
Languages: Català | Deutsch | Español | Français | 한국어 | Interlingua | Italiano | עברית | Latina | Lietuvių | Magyar | Nederlands | 日本語 | Polski | Português | Русский | Simple English | Svenska | Türkçe | Українська | Volapük | 粵語 | 中文
Categories: Cellular automaton rules | Self-organization

 This article needs additional citations for verification.
Please help improve this article by adding reliable references. Unsourced material may be challenged and removed. *(April 2008)*

This article is about the cellular automaton. For the board game, see The Game of Life.

"Conway game" can refer to games as defined by surreal numbers, which Conway also developed.

The **Game of Life** is a cellular automaton devised by the British mathematician John Horton Conway in 1970. It is the best-known example of a cellular automaton.

The "game" is actually a zero-player game, meaning that its evolution is determined by its initial state, needing no input from human players. One interacts with the Game of Life by creating an initial configuration and observing how it evolves.

The location of the page's primary title makes it very clear as to what the content of the page is all about (in this case, Conway's Game of Life). It is good for search engines too, but the content related to this heading is far down the page.

Many of MediaWiki's characteristic links, such as "Edit this page" and "Discuss this page" are again included in this skin underneath the primary content.

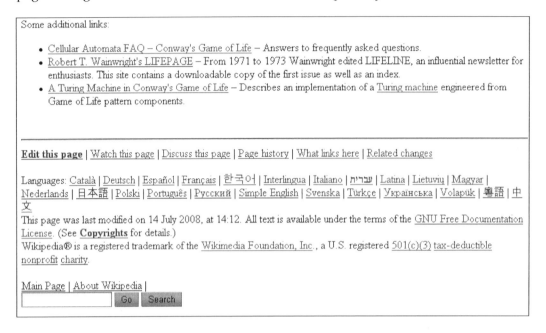

MediaWiki is generally quite slow in presenting pages to the visitors, and the duplication of content in the Nostalgia skin does not prove to be helpful.

Modern

Modern is an improvement on these skins: it looks better-designed, and the muted grays and blues used in the header and navigation help to give the content a greater focus.

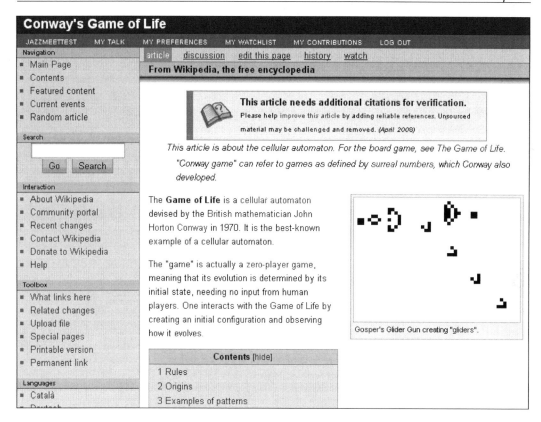

Conway's Game of Life

JAZZMEETTEST   MY TALK   MY PREFERENCES   MY WATCHLIST   MY CONTRIBUTIONS   LOG OUT

article   discussion   edit this page   history   watch

From Wikipedia, the free encyclopedia

This article needs additional citations for verification.
Please help improve this article by adding reliable references. Unsourced material may be challenged and removed. *(April 2008)*

This article is about the cellular automaton. For the board game, see The Game of Life.

"Conway game" can refer to games as defined by surreal numbers, which Conway also developed.

The **Game of Life** is a cellular automaton devised by the British mathematician John Horton Conway in 1970. It is the best-known example of a cellular automaton.

The "game" is actually a zero-player game, meaning that its evolution is determined by its initial state, needing no input from human players. One interacts with the Game of Life by creating an initial configuration and observing how it evolves.

Gosper's Glider Gun creating "gliders".

Contents [hide]
1 Rules
2 Origins
3 Examples of patterns

Notice the absence of the Wikipedia logo in this screenshot. Modern does not allow the space for it, which could present a problem if you want to use your wiki's logo with this skin.

Although the links are not underlined, the "blue" does suggest that visitors can interact with them. Also, the article's content is displayed in a clear manner.

However, but attempting to prove useful for every type of wiki you would want to create, this skin suffers from the same problems as its siblings do. Modern leaves very little to be desired in terms of distinguishing your wiki from other wikis on the Internet. As with MonoBook, Modern's search box is in the left-hand column, meaning it's not instantly recognizable as a search feature, which most users will expect to be at the top right of their screens.

Simple

MediaWiki's Simple skin lives up to its name. Again, the navigation and search features are located in the left-hand column in this skin. But unlike MonoBook and Modern, the "View" links are displayed in this column too, rather than at the top of the page.

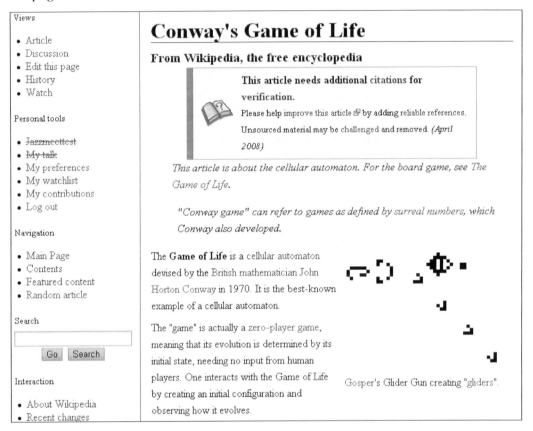

This allows content in the Simple skin to be displayed at the full height of the visitor's browser, which is useful for wikis with long pages of content, such as Wikipedia.

Unlike MonoBook, Simple's category links are not styled so as to separate them from the rest of the content. Instead, they are styled in a similar way to the rest of the page's content, having the same font size but being in blue. This may not be as beneficial for the wiki's visitors, as the centrally-aligned text in the categories box is not as obvious after a long block of left-aligned text. See the following screenshot:

Some additional links:

- Cellular Automata FAQ – Conway's Game of Life ⌖ – Answers to frequently asked questions.
- Robert T. Wainwright's LIFEPAGE ⌖ – From 1971 to 1973 Wainwright edited LIFELINE, an influential newsletter for enthusiasts. This site contains a downloadable copy of the first issue as well as an index.
- A Turing Machine in Conway's Game of Life ⌖ – Describes an implementation of a Turing machine engineered from Game of Life pattern components.

Categories: Cellular automaton rules | Self-organization

Cologne Blue

Cologne Blue follows a format similar to the other MediaWiki skins but has better features. The language links are colored green rather than blue, distinguishing them from the more useful links.

WIKIPEDIA

MAIN PAGE | ABOUT | HELP | FAQ | SPECIAL PAGES | LOG OUT

The Free Encyclopedia

Languages: Català | Deutsch | Español | Français | 한국어 | Interlingua | Italiano | עברית | Latina | Lietuvių | Magyar | Nederlands | 日本語 | Polski | Português | Русский | Simple English | Svenska | Türkçe | Українська | Volapük | 粵語 | 中文

Categories: Cellular automaton rules | Self-organization

Printable version | Disclaimers | Privacy policy

Find

Go | Search

Browse
Main Page
Contents
Featured content
Current events
Random article

Edit
Edit this page
Editing help

This page
Discuss this page
Post a comment
Printable version
Watch this page

Context
Page history
What links here
Related changes

My pages
My page
My talk
My watchlist
My contributions
My preferences
Log out

Special pages

Conway's Game of Life
From Wikipedia, the free encyclopedia

 This article needs additional citations for verification.
Please help improve this article by adding reliable references. Unsourced material may be challenged and removed. *(April 2008)*

This article is about the cellular automaton. For the board game, see The Game of Life.

"Conway game" can refer to games as defined by surreal numbers, which Conway also developed.

The **Game of Life** is a cellular automaton devised by the British mathematician John Horton Conway in 1970. It is the best-known example of a cellular automaton.

The "game" is actually a zero-player game, meaning that its evolution is determined by its initial state, needing no input from human players. One interacts with the Game of Life by creating an initial configuration and observing how it evolves.

Gosper's Glider Gun creating "gliders".

Contents [hide]

1 Rules
2 Origins
3 Examples of patterns

The skin is another dull blur of blue, gray, and blue-gray colors that are most suited to general use.

As we will see, it's useful to skin MediaWiki to help distinguish your wiki and make its useful features stand out.

Customized MediaWiki Skins

An easy option to brighten up your wiki is to change the color scheme of MonoBook. Memory Alpha (http://www.memory-alpha.org) is a good example of the MonoBook skin that uses a different color scheme, but the monotony of MonoBook is still noticeable. However, it does make skinning MediaWiki more rewarding.

Adobe Labs Wiki

The Adobe Labs wiki (http://labs.adobe.com/wiki/) provides information on upcoming technologies at Adobe. It allows the developers to evaluate them before they are fully launched, with information about the application's prerequisite requirements in both hardware and software.

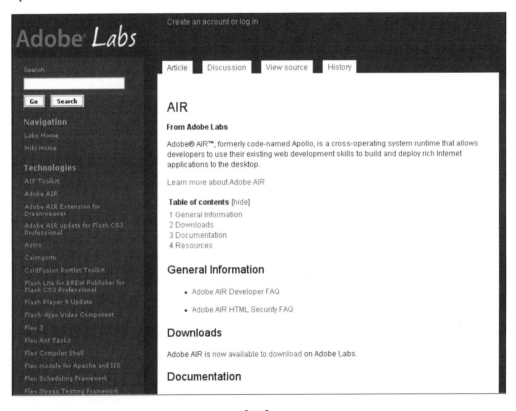

The article content draws focus to itself due to its white background that contrasts with the gray color used in the background and in the column on the left. The article, discussion, view source or edit, and the history links also draw your focus.

In order to edit the articles, visitors must register and log in, as edits by anonymous editors are disabled. Interestingly, visitors can edit articles' discussion pages without the need to register, thus helping to preserve the content of the article with minimal poor quality edits.

The bright red color of the Adobe logo pulls the focus away from the page's main content. Also, the wide column on the left-hand side lessens the width of the article content, thereby diminishing its ability to pull the visitor's eye towards the content.

AboutUs

AboutUs (`http://www.aboutus.org`) is a wiki whose goal is to maintain up-to-date information about other websites and topics or information created by the community. Take a look at the following screenshot:

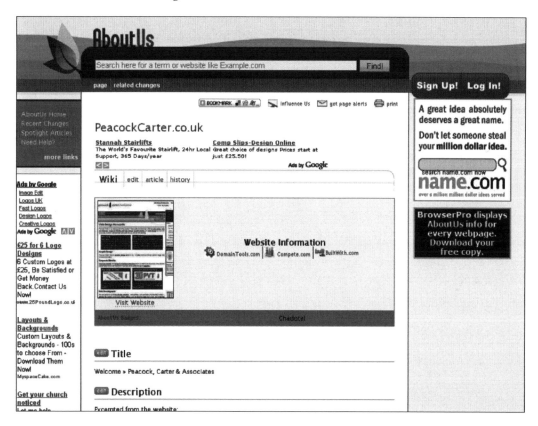

The conspicuous, brightly colored **edit** link is the focus of the page, drawing your attention to the content on the page. Its "make constructive edits anywhere you see fit" encourages short but constructive edits to be made to the articles.

While Wikipedia's more subdued skin buries the **edit** link in the page, **AboutUs** uses color and the positioning of the **edit** feature on the top left to make it incredibly obvious that you can edit the content yourself. Wikipedia may be happy to allow only the more seasoned wiki users to edit content, but as an emerging website, **AboutUs** actively encourages its visitors to contribute to it.

A more careful look at AboutUs reveals the absence of the discussion pages seen on Wikipedia and other wikis. This lessens the number of links required on each page that are not directly related to the page's content, thereby allowing **AboutUs** to appear simpler than Wikipedia.

The **Find** feature presents itself as an "obstacle" to the visitors, thus inviting them to search for the content that they are looking for. The advertising in the right-hand column does not detract from the page's content, and the complementary colors that are used help to make the adverts appear as if they are organic content, rather than a way to generate income for the website.

Another innovation of the **AboutUs** wiki is that it creates the basis of an article on your behalf by locating the domain name's title, and a description extracted from the website.

The WordPress Codex

WordPress (`http://www.wordpress.org`), the blog platform, uses MediaWiki to store its documentation in the WordPress Codex (`http://codex.wordpress.org`).

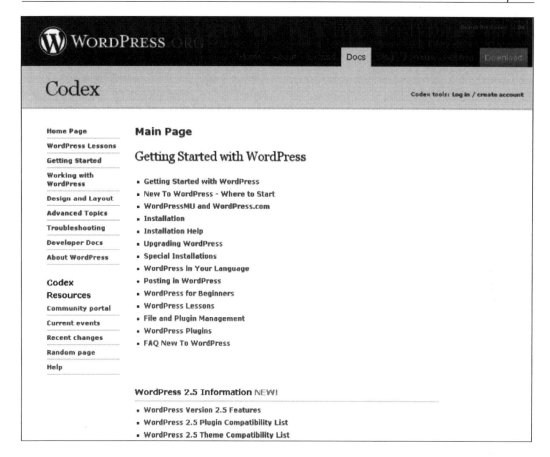

The Codex MediaWiki skin is a vast improvement on MonoBook. The WordPress logo is very attractive. Using a gray header and white text, the logo draws the visitors' attention.

The neutral blue background color for the "sectional" heading "Codex", and the log in and register links towards the right, orientate the visitor to the Codex. These elements help in determining the section of the WordPress website in which we are currently working. They also determine the visitor's ability to log in and even access some other features. The highlighted **Docs** tab in the navigation also helps to orientate the user.

Although the links are not underlined, the blue color indicates that the visitors can click on them. The headings within the page are well-spaced so as to indicate their importance within the page.

Why Skin Your (Media) Wiki?

There are many reasons to skin your MediaWiki wiki. Some of them are as follows:

- **Distinguishing** your wiki's look and feel through your own choice of colors, images, and fonts.

- **Integrating** the wiki with the rest of your website. This can include adding navigation to other areas of your website, or simply copying the design of your main website.

- **Usability** means if your wiki exists for a particular purpose, a custom skin can emphasize the features that are important for the users.

- **Adding widgets** such as advertisements, social media buttons, and other external content, and removing some features of MediaWiki.

We will take a closer look at each of these before moving on to look at our case study.

Distinguishing Your Wiki

Skinning your wiki allows you to distinguish your website from the other websites by using one of the skins supplied with the installation. If your wiki is aimed at a niche usergroup, skinning your wiki can indicate the information in your wiki to the visitors. For example, if your wiki is about tea bags of the nineteenth century, a design that subtly suggests the visitors that the website is about tea bags of the 1800s would prove to be a good idea. In contrast, if you are aiming to create the next Wikipedia, using a skin that features scenes of the French Revolution may not be such a great idea.

The skinning of **AboutUs** does exactly that. It differentiates the wiki from the MonoBook clones that populate the Internet so densely.

Integrating it With Your Website

You can skin your wiki so that it matches the rest of your website. This would prove to be important in business websites that utilize wikis. The reason for this is that reinforcing your brand, including your company logo, name, and color scheme can help the customers in remembering your company. This can aid in providing a smooth transition from where a visitor starts viewing your website to where they obtain the information that they were looking for in your website.

The WordPress Codex is a good example of integrating a wiki into an existing website design.

Improving Your Wiki's Usability

A redesigned wiki can place relevant elements in better positions. When you want to encourage a lot of people to edit your wiki, making the **edit** link the focus of the page will be helpful. When you want to encourage people to discuss articles on your wiki, a more prominent **discussion** link will be helpful. If your wiki articles are short, you will need to add more content in order to make it more readable for the visitors.

Adding and Removing Widgets and Features

Altering your wiki's design is a good idea if you want to incorporate **more features** such as social-bookmarking links so that the visitors can add pages to Digg, Facebook, and Technorati. Skinning MediaWiki will also allow you to remove features such as the discussion page on "AboutUs". Advertising is another feature of 'AboutUs'. It can be added to your wiki so as to help you generate revenue to pay for hosting your wiki.

Our Case Study: JazzMeet

To provide a consistent example throughout this book, we will be skinning MediaWiki for JazzMeet, a wiki used to organise jazz festivals in the same way as BarCamp (`http://www.barcamp.org`) organises meetings to share knowledge. JazzMeet helps in organizing jazz music festivals in various cities across the world, and provides information on the bands and artists performing at each venue, as well as the time and place of every event. Take a look at the following screenshot:

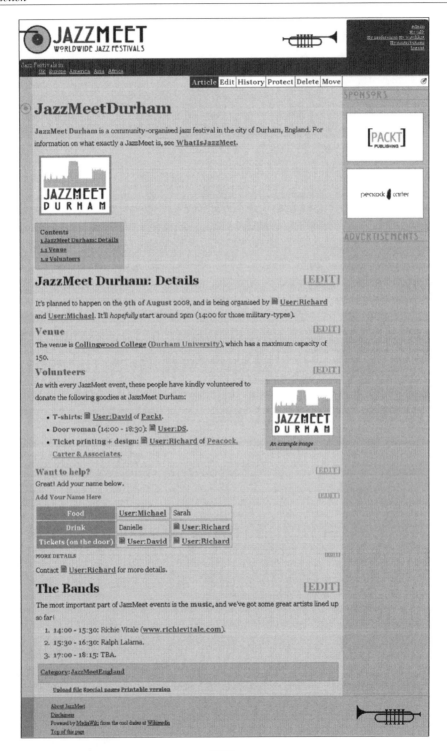

The most noticeable thing about the AboutUs MediaWiki skin is that it doesn't really look like a wiki. The colors create a more welcoming atmosphere than MonoBook's, and whilst there are advertisements, they're generally restricted to the outer columns, well away from the primary content.

The advertisements underneath the page's title are more subtle than the other adverts, adopting the color scheme of the content. The log in and registration links are not as much of a focus, being at the right hand side of the screen, but are still large enough to attract visitors' attention.

A more careful look at AboutUs reveals the absence of the discussion pages seen on Wikipedia and other wikis. This lessens the number of links required on each page that aren't directly related to the page's content, allowing AboutUs to appear simpler than Wikipedia, in turn appearing more inviting to wiki novices.

The search feature presents itself as an 'obstacle' to visitors, inviting them to search for the content they're looking for, and the advertising in the right-hand column doesn't detract from the page's content, but the complementary colors used help to make them feel as if they were organic content, rather than a way to generate income for the website.

Another innovation of the AboutUs wiki - which sadly can't be achieved with skinning - is that following a link to an article which does not exist creates the basis of an article on your behalf, locating the domain name's title, and a description extracted from the website.

The Process of Skinning MediaWiki

Skinning MediaWiki can be a difficult task, but having a way of changing your wiki's appearance methodically can simplify it. The purpose of and the audience for your wiki need to be considered when designing your wiki so as to make it appealing to your audience and to include various desirable features.

Your Wiki's Purpose

Consider the purpose of wiki. For example, will it need a "talk-page" feature, or can we remove this and thereby simplify the wiki's interface for the visitors? Does your wiki really need links to other versions of that page in different languages? It is unlikely if you are just starting your wiki that additional language versions exist. If required, this feature can always be put back at a later date.

If your wiki is primarily for images, a wider content area might be useful to allow the images to be shown in a larger format. If your wiki's content is likely to be text-based, then you need to make the wiki's text easy to read. If your wiki has less text, then you can make the text larger so as to make it easier to read and more prominent on the page.

Try to figure out whether you want your wiki to share documentation, create an encyclopedia, or organize meetings or festivals. Then add (or remove) features from MediaWiki in order to meet the purpose.

Your Wiki's Audience

Your wiki's audience will determine its features to some extent. For example, people in their fifties will probably be less likely to use Digg or Delicious. As a result, adding links for these will be unnecessary in a wiki that is aimed at that age group. If your target audience is an age group that is below fifty, they are more likely to use social bookmarking, so these links may be worth adding.

It is simplest to start with altering the look of your wiki, rather than the layout, and then moving on to add some extra features.

Summary

Wikis are very useful for version management in documents and to share various ideas and information. In recent years, they have grown considerably in use and visibility on the Internet, especially Wikipedia and its sister projects. While the skins that come with the MediaWiki installation are functional, they do not seem to be attractive.

Skinning MediaWiki will also allow you to add and remove features, and style your wiki to match the remainder of your website. This will make it easier to use, and distinguish your wiki from the monotony of MonoBook.

You might have a good idea of what your wiki needs to communicate to your visitors. You also need to consider your wiki's intended audience and purpose. Along with it, you also need to have an idea about the appearance of your wiki.

2
Formatting the Body

In this chapter, we will see how to change the appearance of your wiki. This includes the various content areas of MediaWiki such as the article pages, the edit interface, and the preview interface.

In this chapter, we will cover the following:

- Adding a new skin in MediaWiki, with guidance on setting your new skin as:
    - ° the wiki's default skin
    - ° your default skin
- Styling the article content
- Styling the edit interface
- Styling the preview interface
- Styling the "show changes" interface
- Styling the "log in" and "register" interfaces

Initializing Your Skin

In order to view changes that have made to your skin's design, you need to make a few changes to MediaWiki. We need to inform MediaWiki that we want to view the wiki's content using a different skin from the default, that is, MonoBook.

CSS and Image Files

You will need to create a new directory in the `skins` directory, such as `skins/yourskinname/`, within your MediaWiki installation directory, where `yourskinname` is the name of your new MediaWiki skin.

To keep things simple, we will call our new skin `jazzmeet`, and store it in the `skins/jazzmeet/` directory. The primary Cascading Style Sheets (CSS) file for each skin is usually in this `skin` directory and is known as `main.css`. But it can be changed in the header of your skin's PHP template. For example, the CSS file for our new skin should be located at `skins/jazzmeet/main.css` within our wiki's installation directory.

 You may find it useful to copy an existing skin directory, such as MonoBook (from `skins/monobook/`), and rename it for using it as your new skin's directory (for example, `skins/yourskinname/`).

`shared.css` in `skins/common/` contains styles that are used by all of the skins. We can easily ignore this, as we can overwrite any unwanted style in `main.css`.

PHP Template

We need to carry out the following steps before we can start skinning MediaWiki:

1. Create a PHP file named `YourSkinName.php.` in the `skins/` directory.
2. Open this file and edit the line that reads- `class SkinMonoBook extends SkinTemplate` to read `class YourSkinName extends SkinTemplate`, but replace `YourSkinName` with the name of your new skin.
3. Find the line that reads `class MonoBookTemplate extends QuickTemplate;` to read `class YourSkinNameTemplate extends QuickTemplate;` Again, replace YourSkinName with the name of your new skin.
4. Finally, you need to inform MediaWiki about your skin by inserting the following into the file:

```
$this->skinname   = 'yourskinname'; $this->stylename = 'yourskinname';
$this->template   = 'YourSkinNameTemplate';
```

 The convention in MediaWiki is to name your skin using CamelCase, for example, MonoBook and JazzMeet rather than Monobook and jazzmeet.

Be sure to replace your skin name with the directory's name (for example, `$this->skinname = 'jazzmeet'`), and `YourSkinName` with the name of your new skin as it is in the PHP filename.

 Be careful with variable and directory naming as they are case-sensitive.

Using Your Skin

There are two ways to view your skin: setting it as the default skin for the wiki, and changing your user account preferences, which means that only you will see the skin by default when you are logged in. The latter option means that you will be required to register an account on your wiki after creating an "'admin" or "sysop" account when MediaWiki is installed.

Making Your Skin as Wiki's Default Skin

To make your new skin the default skin for all visitors to your wiki, set the $wgDefaultSkin variable in LocalSettings.php file to the name of your skin. For example, replace $wgDefaultSkin = 'monobook' with $wgDefaultSkin = 'jazzmeet'. Save the file and upload it in its original directory.

 In some versions of MediaWiki, $wgDefaultskin may not be in your LocalSettings.php file. You need to add it if you are not able to see it.

Making Your Skin as Your Default Skin

Log in to your wiki, and select the **my preferences** option from the user bar (positioned at the top-right of the screen in MonoBook). Select the **Skins** tab and you will find your new skin is in the list of skins that are available on your wiki.

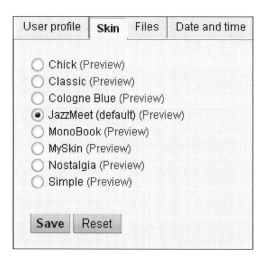

Select the option button that is next to your skin's name, and click the **Save** button at the bottom of the page in order to set the skin as the default each time you log in.

 If you do not have JavaScript enabled, the options in your user account preferences section will be scrambled and will appear as one long page.

Styling Article Content

Now that we can see our new skin, we can start altering its look and feel. If you have copied another skin directory, delete the CSS and image files in the new (copied) directory, so that you are not working with the other CSS that you copied which would undoubtedly result in a bulky and unnecessary CSS.

The Content Body

By default, the content for each page is contained in a div with id `content`, and then CSS rules are applied to `#content`. `#content` does not contain the page's content (this is in `#bodyContent`, which is nested in `#content`), but it contains `.firstHeading`, a `<h1>` tag that holds the page's title.

 If your MediaWiki skin does not follow the naming conventions that are used in the default skins such as MonoBook, you can style your wiki's elements with the help of their references.

There are many elements within `#bodyContent`, each of which has a specific purpose in MediaWiki. Obviously, you can name the elements in your MediaWiki skin as you like, but it would be easier to follow the original naming conventions if you are planning to release the skin for use by other developers.

Category Links

`.catlinks` identifies the container for the different categories in the wiki page. This is similar to Wikipedia's page on Jazz (`http://en.wikipedia.org/wiki/Jazz`). Refer to the following screenshot:

Categories: African American culture | Jazz | Music genres | Musical modernism

editsection: page editing options

`.editsection` distinguishes the "edit" links that are provided against each of the headings in the editable section of the wiki's pages. The following screenshot shows the **edit** option for the section to the right of the heading:

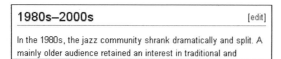

SiteSub: Your Wiki's Claim to Fame

`#siteSub` is used in articles to indicate where the content is from (in a `<h3>` tag). By default, it reads "From YourWikiName". As with `#jump-to-nav`, `#siteSub` is invisible by default in MonoBook.

toc: Table of Contents

`#toc` contains the table of contents. By default, the table of contents appears only when four or more headings exist within the content. `#toc-level1` to `#toclevel6` indicate the hierarchy of the table of contents. A similar example can be viewed at `http://en.wikipedia.org/wiki/Jazz`.

Contents [hide]
1 Origins
2 1890s–1910s
    2.1 Ragtime
    2.2 New Orleans music
3 1920s and 1930s
    3.1 Swing
    3.2 European jazz
4 1940s and 1950s
    4.1 Dixieland revival
    4.2 Bebop
    4.3 Cool jazz
    4.4 Hard bop
    4.5 Free jazz
5 1960s and 1970s
    5.1 Latin jazz
    5.2 Soul jazz
    5.3 Jazz fusion
    5.4 1970s trends
6 1980s–2000s
    6.1 Pop fusion and other subgenres
    6.2 Experimental and straight-ahead performers
7 Definition
8 Improvisation
9 Samples
10 See also
11 Sources
12 References
13 External links

Removing the table of contents:
You can remove the table of contents from MediaWiki pages by inserting the wiki markup __NOTOC__ into the page's editable content.

Wikitable: Tabular Data

wikitable is the default table styling in MediaWiki.

Other elements of interest

#jump-to-nav contains links to enable the visitors to skip to other areas of interest within the current page. In MonoBook, these are hidden with display: none that displays the links when a "user agent" (that is, the browser) does not allow styling with CSS.

#contentSub is used primarily on pages that are redirected to elsewhere on your wiki. They should be left visible as deleting them would make it incredibly difficult to remove a redirect.

Images

When an image is inserted into a wiki page in MediaWiki, the image automatically links to its own uploaded image page. .image classifies the images that are linked to the wiki's content, rather than the images themselves.

Thumbnailed Images

- .thumb, .tright, and .tleft classify images that are thumbnails (created in wiki syntax [[Image:ImagePath.png|thumb|Image caption]]). This (by default) creates an image of 180 pixels wide with the use of inline CSS (CSS that is not in a separate file, but is embedded in the (x) HTML code).

Making Our Case Study 'JazzMeet'

To start altering the look of the JazzMeet wiki, we will begin by altering the style within #content. To make our lives easier, the following colors (in hexadecimal notation) from the JazzMeet concept can be used.

- Dark brown, #38230C, is used to accentuate the "Meet" in "JazzMeet".
- Deep red, #8E1425, is used in the "register" bar.
- Pale beige, #E6E4D8, is used as the background color for the primary content of each page.

- Mid-tone beige, #D9D5C3, is used as the background color for the right-hand column, which contains the sponsors and advertisements.

- Darker beige or brown, #BEB798, is used in image borders and for some <h3> level headings.

Content

Filling your wiki page with adequate content is a better way to check whether every element is taken into account when they are being styled. In the process, it is useful to include the following elements:

- Any one of these headings <h1>, <h2>, <h3>, <h4>, <h5>, and <h6> is preferable, although a <h1> tag is used for the page's title and is assigned the class .firstHeading.

- Images, both without styling and as thumbnails, can be used.

- A table of contents, which is automatically generated when you have four or more headings in a page.

- **Text**: Be sure to include enough text to flow over several lines, especially the text that is bold and italic.

- **Lists**: Both unordered and ordered

- **Links**: In text,
  - A link to a page internal to the wiki which exists
  - A link to a page internal to the wiki which does not exist
  - A link to an external website

- A table of data

- A category (or more) assigned to the wiki page (created by adding [[Category:Category_Name]] to the page in edit mode)

For JazzMeet, a wiki markup is used to create content for the page. You may be more comfortable in creating some dummy content that goes with the theme of your wiki.

```
<!-- this is a comment-->
```

```
'''JazzMeet Durham''' is a community-organised jazz festival in the
city of Durham, England. For information on what exactly a JazzMeet
is, see [[WhatIsJazzMeet]]).
```

```
[[Image:Example.png|An example image]]
```

```
==JazzMeet Durham: Details==
```

It's planned to happen on the '''9th of August''' 2008, and is
being organised by [[User:Richard]] and [[User:Michael]]. It'll
''hopefully'' start around 2pm (14:00 for those military-types).

===Venue===

The venue is [http://www.dur.ac.uk/collingwood Collingwood College]
([http://www.dur.ac.uk Durham University]), which has a maximum
capacity of 150.

===Volunteers===

[[Image:Example.png|thumb|An example image]]

As with every JazzMeet event, these people have kindly volunteered to
donate the following goodies at JazzMeet Durham:

* '''T-shirts''': [[User:David]] of [http://www.packtpub.com Packt].
* '''Door woman''' (14:00 - 18:30): [[User:DS]].
* '''Ticket printing + design''': [[User:Richard]] of [http://www.
peacockcarter.co.uk Peacock, Carter & Associates].

====Want to help?====

Great! Add your name below.

=====Add Your Name Here=====

{| border="1"
|-
! Food
| [[User:Michael]]
| Sarah
|-
! Drink
| Danielle
| [[User:Richard]]
|-
! Tickets (on the door)
| [[User:David]]
| [[User:Richard]]
|}

======More Details======

Contact [[User:Richard]] for more details.

==The Bands==

The most important part of JazzMeet events is the '''music''', and
we've got some great artists lined up so far!

'''14:00 - 15:30''': Richie Vitale ([http://www.richievitale.com
www.richievitale.com]).
'''15:30 - 16:30''': Ralph Lalama.
'''17:00 - 18:15''': TBA.

[[Category:JazzMeetEngland]]

> **Enabling image uploads:**
> In order to enable image uploads in your MediaWiki installation, set
> the value of $wgEnableUploads to true. That is, $wgEnableUploads
> = true.

The Content Block: #content

We will have to apply CSS to #content div in order to style the content body so
as to match our proposed design. At the same time, we will restyle the links in the
content area to match our color scheme. We will make the visited links dark beige,
links that are hovered over as brown, and the non-underlined, and any other link as
red and underlined. The paragraphs in the main content area are given larger text,
and more leading (line-height) to make the content easier to read.

```
#content {
background: #E6E4D8 url("content_bg.gif") repeat-y top left;
color: #000000;
font-family: georgia, "times new roman", times, serif;
padding: 10px 5px 10px 35px;
width: auto;
}
#content p, #content ul, #content ol {
font-size: 100%;
line-height: 175%;
}
#content strong, #content b {
color: #8C1425 !important;
}
#content a, #content a:active, #content a:link {
color: #8C1425;
font-weight: bold;
}
#content a:visited {
color: #857F61;
}
a.text {
border-color: #8C1425;
color: #8C1425;
}
#content a:hover, a:hover.text {
color: #38230C !important;
text-decoration: none !important;
}
```

`#siteSub`, the `<h3>` heading, informs the visitors where the content is from (for example, "From JazzMeet"). This is hidden and is a repetition of some other content on the page. For the same reason, `#jump-to-nav` is also hidden. Although this it is useful for visitors using screen readers, it is a nuisance to those using modern browsers.

```
#siteSub, #jump-to-nav {
display: none;
}
```

MediaWiki differentiates between links of various types by applying classes to them. `a.new` classifies links that lead to another page on the wiki, but that page has not yet been created. `#p-personal` contains user links to their talk page, preferences, and the register and log page, which will be discussed later.

```
a.new, #p-personal a.new {
background: transparent url("a.new.gif") no-repeat top left;
text-decoration: underline;
padding-left: 20px;
}
a.new:visited, #p-personal a.new:visited {
color: #8C1425 !important;
}
.text, .external {
color: #38230C;
}
```

`.external` is used to refer to hyperlinks that go beyond the wiki's namespace (for example, the links created by wiki markup in the following syntax: `[http://www.example.com/ example.com]`).

For an external text link, the XHTML generated is as follows:

```
<a href="http://www.example.com" class="external text"
title="http://www.example.com" rel="nofollow">example.com</a>
```

Thus, the `.text` class classifies text links. Because MediaWiki does not allow external links on images, `text` is used to identify only external text links.

Browser Quirks

To overcome some browser quirks, you have to make use of browser-specific stylesheets. Some of the problems are addressed in MonoBook's CSS fixes, so you can copy the files `IE50Fixes.css`, `IE55Fixes.css`, `IE60Fixes.css`, and `IEMacFixes.css` from `skins/monobook/` to your new skin's directory.

Headings: .mw-headline, .firstHeading

.firstHeading is applied to the <h1> tag, which contains the page's main title. Other headings within the #bodyContent div are classified by the .mw-headline class. The "edit" link is denoted by the .editsection class.

In the case study's design, the page title is displayed in a deep red color (#8D1425) in the typeface "Georgia". We can replace any CSS in the main.css file regarding .firstHeading with the following:

```
h1, .firstHeading {
background: transparent url("firstHeading.gif") center left no-repeat;
border-width: 0;
color: #8D1425;
font-size: 2.2em !important;
font-weight: bold;
margin-bottom: .1em;
margin-left: -35px;
padding-left: 35px;
}
```

Once you have uploaded your new CSS file, refresh your page. The main page heading will now appear in red and, if it is not specified, the font of the content area will now be changed to your browser's default "serif" font.

In the design for JazzMeet, <h2> headings appear in brown color, while other headings appear in dark beige along with smaller text for the headings further down the hierarchy.

```
#content h2, #content h3, #content h4, #content h5, #content h6 {
border-width: 0;
}
h3 .mw-headline, h4 .mw-headline, h5 .mw-headline, h6 .mw-headline {
color: #857F61;
}
h2 .mw-headline {
color: #38230C;
font-size: 120% !important;
font-weight: bold;
}
h3 .mw-headline {
font-size: 120%;
}
h4 .mw-headline {
font-size: 115%;
}
```

```
h5 .mw-headline, h6 .mw-headline {
font-size: 110%;
}
h6 .mw-headline {
text-transform: uppercase;
}
```

Finally, we can change the color of the "edit" link that appears alongside each sectional heading, by applying style to the .editsection class.

```
.editsection {
color: #BEB798 !important;
}
.editsection a, .editsection a:active, .editsection a:link,
.editsection a:visited {
color: #BEB798 !important;
text-transform: uppercase;
}
```

You can render the "edit" link invisible by using display: none. However, this will not stop the visitors from editing your pages if they alter the wiki page's URL from index.php?title= Page_Name to index.php?title=Page_Name&action=edit.

Table Of Contents: #toc, .toc

The table of contents is defined with #toc. It contains an unordered list (<ul>) with links to anchors in the page. Each point in the table of contents is defined in a list item (<li>) tag, and the elements in the list item are separated with <span> tags.

```
<table id="toc" class="toc" summary="Contents"><tr><td>
<div id="toctitle"><h2>Contents</h2></div>
<ul>
<li class="toclevel-1"><a href="#Heading"><span class="tocnumber">1</
span> <span class="toctext">Heading</span></a>
<ul>
<li class="toclevel-2"><a href="#Sub-heading"><span
class="tocnumber">1.1</span> <span class="toctext">Sub-heading</
span></a></li>
</ul>
</li>
<li class="toclevel-1"><a href="#Another_heading"><span
class="tocnumber">2</span> <span class="toctext">Another heading</
span></a></li>
<li class="toclevel-1"><a href="#Another_heading_2"><span
class="tocnumber">3</span> <span class="toctext">Another heading</
span></a></li>
```

```
    </ul>
    </td>
    </tr>
    </table>
```

.toc and #toc apply to the table that surrounds the table of contents. The class applied to the list item itself, .toclevel-x, changes depending on where the heading is placed in the table of contents. Here, 'x' is a number that represents the level of the heading (from 1 to 6). .tocnumber classifies the number of the headings in the table of contents, and .toctext spans the actual text of the heading.

.toctitle defines the div that contains the heading for the table of contents ("Contents"), a <h2> tag. We will align it to the left, so that the toggle link for showing and hiding the table of contents can be floated to the right by defining a style for .toctoggle. In order to match the new skin's color scheme, we will alter the colors of the links, and ensure that the future styling of the table does not affect the table of contents by resetting the border-width attribute to null.

```
#toc, .toc {
border: 1px solid #BEB798 !important;
background: #D9D5C3 !important;
font-size: 75% !important;
margin: 0 10px 10px 0 !important;
padding: 5px !important;
}
#toc h2, .toc h2 {
border-width: 0;
color: #8D1425;
display: inline;
padding: 0;
font-size: 110%;
font-weight: bold;
}
.toc td, .toc th, #toc td, #toc th { /* prevents inheritance of
default #content table styling */
border-width: 0 !important;
}
#toc #toctitle, .toc #toctitle, #toc .toctitle, .toc .toctitle {
text-align: left;
}
#toc ul, .toc ul {
list-style-type: none;
list-style-image: none;
margin: 0;
padding: 0;
```

```
text-align: left;
}
#toc ul ul, .toc ul ul {
margin: 0 0 0 5px;
}
#toc #toctitle, .toc #toctitle, #toc .toctitle, .toc .toctitle {
text-align: left;
}
#toc .toctoggle, .toc .toctoggle {
display: inline;
font-size: 90% !important;
float: right;
text-transform: uppercase;
}
#toc a, #toc a:active, #toc a:link, #toc a:visited {
color: #8D1425;
}
```

Another option for the table of contents is to render it invisible through the use of `.toc, #toc {display: none}`.

 Beware that pages containing __TOC__ (to force the page to show a table of contents), will not show a table of contents if you do this.

Categories

MediaWiki allows pages to be assigned to one or more "categories", much like bloggers can "tag" their articles with different keywords. `.catlinks` classifies this content, which only appears on a page when a page has been assigned to one or more categories. This can be done by adding `[[Category:CategoryName]]` to the page.

In order to match the case study's color scheme, we can restyle the category links div to a darker beige color and using a border to make it distinct from the remainder of the content area. The text is made slightly smaller, as it is not likely to be prime content for most of our visitors.

```
#catlinks {
border: 1px solid #BEB798;
background: #D9D5C3;
font-size: 85%;
padding: 5px;
margin: 10px 5px;
clear: both;
}
```

The link colors for the "category" block will be inherited from the ones that are specified for the links in `#content`.

Images

There are two methods for inserting images into a wiki page with wiki markup. Firstly, only `[[Image:ImageName.jpg|Image description]]` can be used. This inserts the image in to the page and assigns it to the `.image` class. Secondly, the `[[Image:ImageName.jpg|thumb|Image description]]` or `[[Image:ImageName.jpg|thumb|left|Image description]]` syntax can be used to insert the image `ImageName.jpg`.

The images in the JazzMeet concept are floated, but this is achieved by using inline CSS in the wiki page. If you attempt to float images in `#content` or `#bodyContent`, you will realize that it causes difficulties on other pages, including the redirect pages. However, we will still give a beige-colored border to the images..

```
.image img {
border: 5px #BEB798 solid;
margin: 10px;
max-width: 500px;
}
.thumb .image {
border-width: 0;
}
```

This gives the maximum width to an image which prevents the image from covering other content (such as the right-hand column) if an over-sized image is uploaded and added to a page. It also removes the border from the image thumbnail, since we want thumbnails to appear different to normal images.

Thumbnail Images

The thumbnail XHTML is reasonably complex. It has the capacity to hold the caption for the image, as well as an icon that links to the full-size version of the image.

By default, thumbnail images float to the right (inherited from the `.tright` class), but the position of the image on the page can be overridden by the user with the syntax `[[Image:ImageName.jpg|thumb|left|Image description]]`. This replaces the `.tright` class with the `.tleft` class. Refer to the following code:

```
.tright {
clear: right;
float: right;
margin: 5px 0 5px 10px;
}
.tleft {
clear: left;
float: left;
margin: 5px 10px 5px 0;
}
```

For the JazzMeet wiki, thumbnails need to be restyled in order to coordinate them with the rest of the content.

```
.thumb {
background: #D9D5C3;
border: 1px #BEB798 solid;
padding: 5px;
width: auto;
}
.thumb .image img {
border: 1px #BEB798 solid;
width: 140px;
}
.thumbcaption {
font-size: 80% !important;
font-style: italic;
padding: 0 5px !important;
}
```

We can also change the styling of the "magnify" image that links to the larger image, by altering both .magnify and .magnify img.

```
.magnify {
float: left;
width: auto;
}
.magnify img {
float: left;
width: auto;
}
```

You can change the "magnify" image to match your skin's theme by replacing (or creating) a file called magnify-clip.png in the skins/common/images/ directory. Browsers such as Internet Explorer and Firefox need to be told that the image should not be displayed with a border around it.

```
.magnify img, .magnify img a {
border-width: 0 !important;
}
```

This styles the thumbnails in a manner similar to the one in MonoBook, but in the JazzMeet color scheme, as shown in the following screenshot. Note that the "magnify" icon in the bottom right of the thumbnail has not been altered:

Tables

At this point, the tables on your test wiki page are likely to be styled with your browser's default styling. We can coordinate the styling of the tables in the content area with the remainder of the page's content. Refer to the following code:

```
#content table {
background: transparent;
border-width: 0;
}
#content th, #content td {
padding: 5px;
}
#content th {
background: #BEB798;
border-width: 0;
color: #FFFFFF;
font-weight: bold;
}
#content td {
border: 1px #BEB798 solid;
}
#content caption {
display: none;
}
```

This gives a very simple default style for the tables. Wiki markup allows users to restyle tables to some extent.

Talk Pages

A few changes need to be made so as to alter the talk page and message notifications that appear at the top of wiki pages when a user is logged in and receives a new message on their talk page.

New Message Notification: .usermessage

`.usermessage` classifies the div that appears when a new message is received on a user's talk page.

```
.usermessage {
background: #D9D5C3 url("usermessage.gif") top left no-repeat;
border: 2px #8D1425 solid;
color: black;
font-weight: bold;
margin: 2em 0 1em;
padding: 15px 5px 15px 60px;
vertical-align: middle;
}
```

After uploading the CSS and placing a suitable image, `errormessage.gif` in the skin folder, a message box is produced on your talk page as seen in the following image:

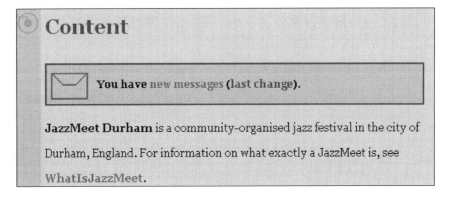

Redirect Pages

Redirect pages are partially styled through the application of the CSS previously mentioned, but you can address the content of redirect pages on MediaWiki with the use of the `.redirectText` class. The only text that appears on redirect pages is the name of the page, so we'll make the text easier to read by enlarging it.

```
.redirectText {
font-size: 175%;
}
```

You can specify an image to display beside the name of the page. This can be done either by creating an image or by replacing the image in the skins/common/images/ directory named redirectltr.png. (For the sake of consistency, you could replace redirectrtl.png too).

Image Detail Pages

An image detail page displays a full-size image in an article. Most of our work in styling this page will be already done if #content has been styled. #filetoc, an unordered list, contains the table of contents for the uploaded media pages. It can also be altered so as to match the rest of the wiki. Refer to the following code:

```
ul#filetoc {
border: 1px solid #aaaaaa;
background: #D9D5C3;
border: 1px #BEB798 solid;
font-size: 90%;
margin: 10px;
padding: 5px;
}
#filetoc li {
display: inline;
list-style-type: none;
margin: 5px;
}
h2#filelinks {
color: #857F61;
font-weight: bold;
text-transform: uppercase;
}
```

Some pages in the wiki that make use of the image are listed, and this header can be styled by applying CSS to h2#filelinks.

```
h2#filelinks {
color: #857F61;
font-weight: bold;
text-transform: uppercase;
}
```

Empty Articles

A message appears when you visit a non-existent URL within the wiki's namespace, by typing the page's address manually into your browser's address bar. This message does not appear if you follow a link to an article that does not exist. In that case, you are redirected to the edit interface to begin creating the page.

This message can be styled using `div.noarticletext`. If the message appears on the screen, it means that not much text is on the page. We can therefore make the message more prominent by enlarging the text.

```
.noarticletext {
font-size: 150%;
}
```

Search Results

As search results are paginated, you can style the elements that appear in the search results page (`Special:Search`) by addressing them directly, and by making use of the unique class name assigned to each page's `<body>` tag in the wiki `.page-Special_Search`.

Recent Changes

Similarly, the recent changes page (`Special:Recentchanges`) needs no alteration to finish skinning it, but can be styled by reference to `.page-Special_Recentchanges`.

Styling the Edit Interface

The edit interface appears when you select the "edit" option at the top of the page. It allows visitors to edit the page's content in your wiki by using a mixture of wiki markup and inline CSS. Now that the article interface has been styled, little needs to be styled to alter the appearance of the edit interface.

The Basics

The edit interface is contained within a `<form>`, which can be styled to differentiate it from the general content.

```
#content form {
background: #D9D5C3;
border: 1px solid #BEB798;
margin: 3px 0;
padding: 10px 5px;
}
```

There are a number of elements contained within the edit interface form. These are as follows:

- #wpSummary is the text box that is used to describe the nature of the edit made by the wiki's visitor.

- #wpMinorEdit is a check-box that indicates whether the associated edit to the page was "minor" (that is, small changes). pWatchthis is another check box that allows a user to specify whether the page is to be listed in their "watchlist". The watchlist feature is only available to the users who are registered and logged in.

- #wpSave is a submit button that saves the changes the user has made to the page, so that other users of the wiki can view your changes with immediate effect.

- #wpPreview is a button that allows the user to preview your page. MediaWiki generates a version of the page as it would appear if the changes were saved, but does not actually save the changes.

- Finally, #wpDiff is a button that allows the user to see the difference between the last version of the page and the changes that they have made.

It is better not to define the width and the height for the <textarea> (#wpTextbox1) used to edit the wiki, because the columns and rows are defined in XHTML. There are still some small changes that can be made to help style the text area in order to match your skin, such as altering the borders and changing the background colors.

One of the most useful aspects of skinning MediaWiki is the ability to use proportional font sizes in the text area. This would be of a great help to those with disabilities, especially visually impaired persons, as it makes the editing of the content easier.

```
#wpTextbox1 {
font-family: georgia, "times new roman", times, sans-serif;
font-size: 100%;
}
```

The background and borders are defined together with the style for the other elements in the form, so as to minimize the CSS file size. The text boxes and check boxes still need styling, as do the background color and border of the text area.

```
#wpTextbox1, #wpSummary, #wpMinoredit, #wpWatchthis {
background: #E6E4D8;
border: 1px solid #BEB798;
margin: 5px 0;
}
```

The buttons at the bottom of the form are contained within .editbuttons for ease of movement, and they appear a little close to the other elements in the form. Now, we will add some space above and below them.

```
.editbuttons {
margin: 10px 0;
}
```

The "Save", "Preview", and "Diff" (difference) buttons contained within .editbuttons can now be styled to match the remaining elements in the form.

```
#wpSave, #wpDiff {
font-weight: normal;
}
#wpSave, #wpDiff {
background: #E6E4D8;
border: 2px solid #BEB798;
color: #38230C; /* brown */
padding: 3px 5px;
}
#wpPreview {
background: #8D1425;
border: 2px #FFFFFF solid;
color: #FFFFFF;
font-weight: bold;
padding: 3px 5px;
}
```

The 'Preview' button appears in red in order to encourage JazzMeet's visitors to preview their page before saving it, and thereby reduce the number of useless edits being made to the wiki. To help accentuate the "preview" button, we can move the "cancel" and "editing help" links beneath the .editbuttons div.

```
.editHelp {
display: block;
font-size: 75%;
margin: 5px 0;
}
```

The "edit" interface will now look similar to the following image:

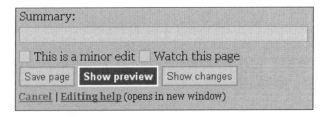

Toolbar

You may want to limit what you change in the toolbar, as many of your visitors will already be familiar with the toolbar-based text editor on the web. You may be expecting something similar to be displayed on your website as well. Similar to the rest of MediaWiki's markup, the "edit" interface's toolbar has a unique identifying value (#toolbar).

If you want to alter the toolbar's images, you can replace the images prefixed with button_ in skins/common/images/.

 Before replacing the toolbar button images, remember to create a copy of them elsewhere, in case you want to restore them at a later stage.

Legal Notices and Warnings

#editpage-copywarn contains a warning that is displayed on the edit interface's page, thereby notifying the users that the content they submit to the wiki may be "edited mercilessly", and a reminder not to submit the copyrighted work. For JazzMeet, we will decrease the size of the text to help retain a friendly atmosphere for visitors.

```
#editpage-copywarn {
color: #202020;
font-size: 75%;
}
```

Preview Page

The "Preview" page acts as an interpretation of what the page you are currently editing would look like if you were to save it. The preview is placed above the edit interface so that you can make changes to the article after previewing it.

As the styling has done most of the work for us, there are only two elements of the preview page that still need to be covered. They are: previewnote, a reminder that any changes made to the page have not been saved, and #wikiPreview, the containing div for the preview.

Knowing how forgetful people can be, we can style this section to be more distinguished than it is in MonoBook, with a deep red border with a width of 2 pixels. We will also set the message that reminds us that we are only viewing the preview a little larger than other text.

```
#wikiPreview {
border: 2px #8D1425 solid !important;
padding: 0;
}
.previewnote {
color: #8D1425;
font-size: 150%;
}
```

The preview page will now appear a bit different from the normal page view, which will hopefully prevent any cases of edits being lost because the visitors thought they had submitted their edits rather than just previewed them.

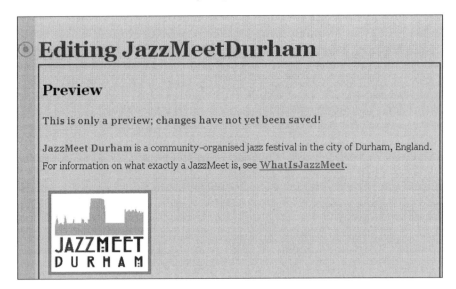

 The edit page's template includes #wikiPreview by default, so any ambitious styling may affect the appearance of your edit page and preview page.

Show Differences

If you select the "Show Changes" option from the edit interface, you will see two columns: one that contains the last version of the page's content, and one that shows the version of the content (which has not yet been saved).

When displayed in the JazzMeet skin, the "show changes" view is displayed in two table columns alongside each other. Areas of changed content are highlighted in yellow cells in the left-hand column. Content that has been added is highlighted red, with the relevant portion of content being highlighted with a green background.

Editing JazzMeetDurham

Current revision	Your text
Line 6:	**Line 6:**
It's planned to happen on the '''9th of August''' 2008, and is being organised by [[User:Richard]] and [[User:Michael]]. It'll "hopefully" start around 2pm (14:00 for those military-types).	It's planned to happen on the '''9th of August''' 2008, and is being organised by [[User:Richard]] and [[User:Michael]]. It'll "hopefully" start around 2pm (14:00 for those military-types).
===Venue===	
The venue is [http://www.dur.ac.uk/collingwood Collingwood College] ([http://www.dur.ac.uk Durham University]), which has a maximum capacity of 150.	The venue is [http://www.dur.ac.uk/collingwood Collingwood College] ([http://www.dur.ac.uk Durham University]), which has a maximum capacity of 150.
Line 13:	**Line 11:**
===Volunteers===	===Volunteers===
[[Image:Example.png|thumb|An example image]]	[[Image:Example.png|thumb|An example image]] Added text.
As with every JazzMeet event, these people have kindly volunteered to donate the following goodies at JazzMeet Durham:	As with every JazzMeet event, these people have kindly volunteered to donate the following goodies at JazzMeet Durham:

`.diff-otitle` is used to identify the table cell that contains the heading for the current version of the page, as saved in the wiki's database. Similarly, `.diff-ntitle` identifies the table cell that contains the heading for the version of the page's content in the edit box. To highlight these cells, we will make them bold, and change their colors.

```
.diff-otitle, .diff-ntitle {
background: #BEB798 !important;
color: #FFFFFF;
font-weight: bold;
}
```

The cells (`<td>`) that indicate the lines of the content's wiki markup are identified by `.diff-lineno`.

```
td.diff-lineno {
color: #BEB798;
}
```

`.diff-context` classifies the cells containing the content that surrounds the changed areas in them. `.diff-marker` identifies cells that give hints to the visitor about the content, including the cells containing a "+" or "-" to indicate whether content has been added or removed from that area. The cells containing line numbers (`.diff-lineno`) can also be styled by applying CSS. Because these cells are not as important as the content being changed in this table, we will give them a beige background.

```
.diff-context, .diff-marker {
background: #D9D5C3 !important;
}
```

`.diff-deletedline` classifies the table cells that contain a line that is present in the current page, but is now being deleted by the user. `.diff-addedline`, originally, classifies the content that has been inserted compared to the current version.

Lastly, `.diffchange` identifies the area of the text that has been added to the current version. It looks fine in its default red, but we will style it to become our 'JazzMeet' beige instead.

```
.diffchange {
color: #BEB798 !important;
}
```

Although these changes have only styled a small portion of the wiki, they will help to integrate the skin fully across the wiki. If the elements are not styled as consistently as they were in MonoBook, we will have a very poor skin.

Editing JazzMeetDurham

Current revision	Your text
Line 6:	Line 6:
It's planned to happen on the '''9th of August''' 2008, and is being organised by [[User:Richard]] and [[User:Michael]]. It'll "hopefully" start around 2pm (14:00 for those military-types).	It's planned to happen on the '''9th of August''' 2008, and is being organised by [[User:Richard]] and [[User:Michael]]. It'll "hopefully" start around 2pm (14:00 for those military-types).
-	
- ===Venue===	
The venue is [http://www.dur.ac.uk/collingwood Collingwood College] ([http://www.dur.ac.uk Durham University]), which has a maximum capacity of 150.	The venue is [http://www.dur.ac.uk/collingwood Collingwood College] ([http://www.dur.ac.uk Durham University]), which has a maximum capacity of 150.
Line 13:	Line 11:
===Volunteers===	===Volunteers===
- [[Image:Example.png|thumb|An example image]]	+ [[Image:Example.png|thumb|An example image]] Added text.
As with every JazzMeet event, these people have kindly volunteered to donate the following goodies at JazzMeet Durham:	As with every JazzMeet event, these people have kindly volunteered to donate the following goodies at JazzMeet Durham:

Logging In and Registering

The login and registration pages are mostly styled by this stage, but you may want to tidy them up a bit. In the JazzMeet skin, the table that holds the login form inherits the default table styling given in the content area.

The login form can be identified by `#userloginForm`, so we can remove the borders. The registration page also displays the table cell borders around elements in our form, so the borders need to be removed from the table elements in the `#userlogin2` div.

```
#userloginForm table, #userloginForm th, #userloginForm td,
#userlogin2 table, #userlogin2 td, #userlogin2 th {
border-width: 0 !important;
}
```

#wpName1 and #wpPassword1 are text boxes that contain the username and password respectively, of the visitor attempting to log in. #wpLoginattempt and #wpMailmypassword identify the input elements that allow a visitor to attempt to log in with their entered username and password, and have their password emailed to them if the have forgotten it, respectively. We have previously styled the input boxes and submit buttons for the edit interface, so we can just add the relevant identifiers to the original CSS.

```
#wpSave, #wpDiff,
#wpName1, #wpPassword1 {
background: #E6E4D8;
border: 2px solid #BEB798;
color: #38230C;
padding: 3px 5px;
}
#wpSave, #wpDiff,
#wpLoginattempt, #wpMailmypassword  {
background: #E6E4D8;
border: 2px solid #BEB798;
color: #38230C;
padding: 3px 5px;
}
```

The check box on the login page (classified by #wpRemember) can also be styled, but it is not necessary for JazzMeet.

JazzMeets So Far

So far, we have an attractive page body, with little or no styling for the surrounding content such as the userbar, the search box, and the footer information. We will look at these elements in subsequent chapters. For now, our pages will appear as shown in the example below:

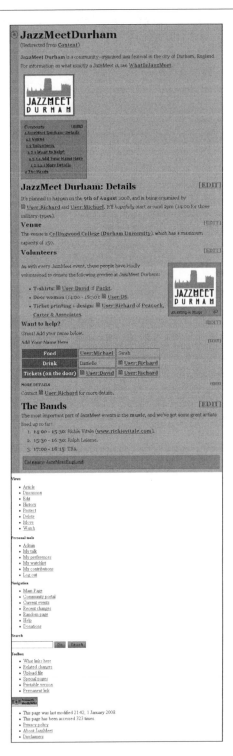

If you are reworking your skin from MonoBook's CSS, you may notice that some elements such as the column navigation and search feature hover over your page. This is due to the positioning within the CSS that has not yet been overwritten or removed. It may be easier to work on your skin if you comment out the CSS applied to these elements from your stylesheet.

Summary

In this chapter, we have discussed how to style the content section of the wiki. We have covered the following:

- Elements needed to style for the page's main content
- Styling the edit interface
- Styling the preview interface and the show changes interface
- Styling the file details pages
- Styling redirect pages
- Styling the log in and registration interfaces

In the next few chapters, we will learn how to style the area surrounding the main content area, and change the layout of your wiki.

3
Formatting Interface Elements

Our wiki's content is now skinned, but there is still a lot of work to be done to style and change the layout of the remaining skin. We need to work on the area around the content block, such as the userbar, the main website navigation, and the links to various tools for manipulating the information on the wiki page. In this chapter, we will cover the following:

- Changing your wiki's logo
- Styling the wiki's navigation
- Styling your wiki's userbar elements, for example, the "log in" and "register" links
- Styling your wiki's page option links, for example, 'edit', and 'discussion'
- Styling your wiki's toolbox
- Altering the search feature
- Changing the footer

The Interface Area: .portlet

The area around the main content area is classified by the `.portlet` class. Beware of excessively styling this, because by default, the class includes the page's userbar, its navigation, and the search facility. We can either change the classes applied to these files in our MediaWiki skin's PHP template file, or work with the classes and ids used in other MediaWiki themes such as MonoBook.

We have already declared our chosen fonts for the content area, but we can redefine the fonts for the areas surrounding the content. Refer to the following code:

```
.portlet {
font-family: georgia, "times new roman", times, serif;
}
```

Changing the Logo

One of the most obvious things that can be done to alter the appearance of your wiki is to change the logo. The following ways can be used to achieve this in MediaWiki:

- Changing the logo image located at `skins/common/images/wiki.png`
- Changing the `$wgLogo` parameter in the `LocalSettings.php` file (in the root directory of your MediaWiki installation)
- Adding the relevant XHTML to your skin's PHP file (for example, `skins/ JazzMeet.php`)

The Logo File

In MonoBook, the logo is not inserted as an `<img>` element directly in to the XHTML. It is set as a background image through the use of inline CSS.

```
<div class="portlet" id="p-logo">
<a style="background-image: url(<?php $this->text('logopath') ?>);"
<?php ?>href="<?php echo htmlspecialchars($this->data['nav_urls']
['mainpage']['href'])?>"<?php echo
$skin->tooltipAndAccesskey('n-mainpage') ?>></a>
</div>
```

The default size for logo images is 135 pixels by 135 pixels. This is the universal size that is been used for all the default skins that are supplied with MediaWiki.

MediaWiki assumes that the logo is in Portable Network Graphic (PNG) format, although this can be altered.

 Portable Network Graphics with a transparent background will not be displayed as intended in Internet Explorer 6.

Of course, with JazzMeet, we will need the logo to be of a different size than the default, as it is rectangular rather than square.

This can be achieved by specifying our own XHTML in JazzMeet's PHP skin template file.

Changing Your Logo in the PHP File

Your wiki's logo can be changed in the PHP template file, stored in `skins/`. We called this file `JazzMeet.php`. Find the `#p-logo` div in this file.

```
<div class="portlet" id="p-logo">
<a style="background-image: url(<?php $this->text('logopath') ?>);"
<?php?>href="<?php echo htmlspecialchars($this->data['nav_urls']['main
page']['href'])?>"<?php
        echo $skin->tooltipAndAccesskey('n-mainpage') ?>>
</a>
</div>
```

Replace the content within this div with your own logo XHTML. For JazzMeet, this will be as follows:

```
<div class="portlet" id="p-logo">
<a href="http://www.jazzmeet.com/" title="JazzMeet">
<img src="skins/jazzmeet/jazzmeet-logo.png" alt="JazzMeet logo" />
</a>
</div>
```

 Replacing the logo in the way just mentioned means that only visitors who are using your wiki's custom skin will be able to see it. If you allow visitors to select other skins, they will not see your wiki's custom logo.

Changing the Logo in LocalSettings.php: $wgLogo

To change your wiki's logo using the `LocalSettings.php` file, find the line that begins with `$wgLogo`, and replace its value with the path to your logo image, relative to the root directory of your MediaWiki install. Alternatively, you can specify an absolute path, such as this: `http://www.example.com/wiki/skins/jazzmeet/logo.png`.

For example, if your wiki has been installed in `www.example.com/wiki/`, and your logo file is in `www.example.com/wiki/skins/jazzmeet/logo.png`, the code in the `LocalSettings.php` file should be as follows:

```
## Logo file to add (called in TemplateName.php)
$wgLogo = "skins/jazzmeet/logo.png";
```

Changing the Logo File

By replacing the logo file, `wiki.png`, in the `skins/common/images/` directory, you can instantly change your wiki's logo. This directory is the default location for the wiki's logo, which is used even if the `$wgLogo` parameter in the `LocalSettings.php` file is not set.

Styling the Navigation: #p-navigation

`#p-navigation` identifies the div that contains the `<h5>` header above the navigation links, and `.pBody`, which includes an unordered list of wiki-wide navigation links. `.pBody` is used elsewhere, so as to avoid unnecessary styling.

- Main Page
- Community portal
- Current events
- Recent changes
- Random page
- Help
- Donations

Table of Elements: #p-navigation

Each list item in the main navigation div has a unique id assigned to it:

Element class/id	Purpose
#p-navigation	#p-navigation identifies the container for the wiki's primary navigation.
#n-mainpage	#n-mainpage identifies the list item containing a link to the wiki's main page.
#n-portal	#n-portal identifies the list item containing a link to the wiki's portal page.
#n-currentevents	#n-currentevents identifies the list item containing a link to the wiki's current events page.
#n-recentchanges	#n-recentchanges identifies the list item containing a link to the recent changes page, which lists the most recent edits made to your wiki.
#n-randompage	#n-randompage identifies the list item containing a link to an existing page in your wiki, chosen at random each time the link is clicked.
#n-help	#n-help identifies the list item containing a link to your wiki's help topics.
#n-sitesupport	#n-sitesupport identifies the list item containing a link to a page where your visitors can make a donation to help pay the running costs of your wiki.

#p-navigation contains more than an unordered list of links that acts as the wiki's main navigation:

```
<div class='portlet' id='p-navigation'>

<h5>Navigation</h5>

<div class='pBody'>

<ul>
    <li id="n-mainpage"><a href="/yourwiki/Main_Page" title="Visit the
Main Page [z]" accesskey="z">Main Page</a></li>
    <li id="n-portal"><a href="/yourwiki/JazzMeet:Community_
Portal" title="About the project, what you can do, where to find
things">Community portal</a></li>
    <li id="n-currentevents"><a href="/yourwiki/Current_events"
title="Find background information on current events">Current events</
a></li>
    <li id="n-recentchanges"><a href="/yourwiki/Special:
Recentchanges" title="The list of recent changes in the wiki. [r]"
accesskey="r">Recent changes</a></li>
```

```
    <li id="n-randompage"><a href="/yourwiki/Special:Random"
title="Load a random page [x]" accesskey="x">Random page</a></li>
    <li id="n-help"><a href="/yourwiki/Help:Contents" title="The place
to find out.">Help</a></li>
    <li id="n-sitesupport"><a href="/yourwiki/JazzMeet:Site_support"
title="Support us">Donations</a></li>
</ul>

</div>

</div>
```

 Noticeably, the design for JazzMeet does not include the main navigation links as MonoBook does. This is because features such as the "random article" link and "community portal" are not needed for JazzMeet.

The Userbar: #p-personal

In the Western world, MediaWiki's userbar is displayed in the top right of your screen by default in MonoBook, (and in the top left of the screen for those countries who read from the right to the left). It is classified with the #p-personal div.

```
<div class="portlet" id="p-personal">

<h5>Personal tools</h5>

<div class="pBody">
<ul>
    <li id="pt-userpage"><a href="/yourwiki/User:Admin" title="My user
page [.]" accesskey=".">Admin</a></li>
    <li id="pt-mytalk"><a href="/yourwiki/User_talk:Admin" title="My
talk page [n]" accesskey="n">My talk</a></li>
    <li id="pt-preferences"><a href="/yourwiki/Special:Preferences"
title="My preferences">My preferences</a></li>
    <li id="pt-watchlist"><a href="/yourwiki/Special:Watchlist"
title="The list of pages you're monitoring for changes [l]"
accesskey="l">My watchlist</a></li>
    <li id="pt-mycontris"><a href="/yourwiki/Special:Contributions/
Admin" title="List of my contributions [y]" accesskey="y">My
contributions</a></li>
    <li id="pt-logout"><a href="/yourwiki/index.php?title=Special:Userl
ogout&amp;returnto=JazzMeetDurham" title="Log out">Log out</a></li>
</ul>

</div>

</div>
```

Table of Elements: #p-personal

Element class/id	Purpose
`#p-personal`	`#p-personal` identifies the container for the userbar.
`#pt-userpage`	`#pt-userpage` identifies the list item containing a link to the user's userpage, if the user is logged in to an account.
`#n-mytalk`	`#pt-mytalk` identifies the list item containing a link to the user's talk (discussion) page, if the user is logged in.
`#pt-preferences`	`#pt-preferences` identifies the list item containing a link to the user's preferences and settings, if the user if logged in.
`#pt-watchlist`	`#pt-watchlist` identifies the list item containing a link to the user's list of currently-watched pages, if the user is logged in.
`#pt-mycontris`	`#pt-mycontris` identifies the list item containing a link to the user's contributions to the wiki.
`#pt-logout`	`#pt-logout` identifies the list item containing a link to log out of the user's account.
`#pt-login`	`#pt-login` identifies the list item of the link to the log in interface where `#pt-anonlogin` is not used.
`#pt-anonuserpage`	`#pt-anonuserpage` identifies the list item containing a link to an anonymous user page, if you are not logged in to the wiki.
`#pt-anontalk`	`#pt-anontalk` identifies the list item containing a link to the user's IP address' discussion (talk) page, if the user is not logged in.
`#pt-anonlogin`	`#pt-anonlogin` identifies the list item containing a link to the log in interface.

- Admin
- My talk
- My preferences
- My watchlist
- My contributions
- Log out

Most websites' userbars are positioned to the top right of the visitor's screen. Consequently, this is the first place where your wiki's visitors are likely to look for this feature on your website. So, moving it to another location could make it less obvious to your wiki's visitors that they are logged in, or even that there is an option to register and contribute.

#p-personal and its contents will eventually need moving within the JazzMeet.
php file to put it in the position we want. We can style the colors to match our new
skin's color scheme, and change the background image to give it a more rounded
appearance at the top.

```
#p-personal {
background: #8D1425 url("p-personal_bg.png") no-repeat top right;
color: #FFFFFF;
float: right; /* To position it */
height: 165px;
padding: 10px;
width: 170px;
}
#p-personal ul {
list-style-type: none;
margin: 0;
padding: 0;
font-size: 75%;
text-align: right;
}
    #p-personal li {
    display: inline;
    }
    #p-personal a {
    color: #FFFFFF;
    }
```

Because this crams all of the user's options into a small box, it is hard to distinguish
between the options. So, we can split some on to new lines in an effort to "group"
them where they will be of more use to JazzMeet's visitors.

To help differentiate these options, we can split the options in to four distinct rows:

- The user's homepage link (**Admin**)
- The **My talk** and **My preferences** links
- **My contributions**
- **Log out**

The simplest way to split these options is to use display: block to create a new line
for the first listed item of the new line.

```
#pt-mytalk, #pt-contris, #pt-logout,
#pt-anontalk, #pt-anonlogin {
display: block;
}
```

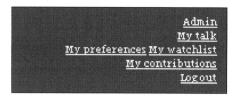

If you log out, the log-in link is more prominently displayed than the other options, to encourage JazzMeet's visitors to contribute to the wiki:

View Options: #p-cactions

`#p-cactions` defines the containing div for the page's viewing options, including the article, edit, discussion, and page history links. It also includes links to block the editing of a page and move the page for users with administrator or system operator status.

- Article
- Discussion
- Edit
- History
- Protect
- Delete
- Move
- Watch

To view all available options, it is useful to log in to an admin account, which will display every item that needs to be considered.

```
<div id="p-cactions" class="portlet">
<h5>Views</h5>
<div class="pBody">
<ul>
    <li id="ca-nstab-main" class="selected"><a href="/yourwiki/
index.php/JazzMeetDurham" title="View the content page [c]"
accesskey="c">Article</a></li>
    <li id="ca-talk"><a href="/yourwiki/index.php/Talk:JazzMeetDurham"
title="Discussion about the content page [t]" accesskey="t">Discussio
n</a></li>
```

```
    <li id="ca-edit"><a href="/yourwiki/index.php?title=JazzMeetDurham&
amp;action=edit" title="You can edit this page. Please use the preview
button before saving. [e]" accesskey="e">Edit</a></li>
    <li id="ca-history"><a href="/yourwiki/index.php?title=JazzMeet
Durham&amp;action=history" title="Past versions of this page. [h]"
accesskey="h">History</a></li>
    <li id="ca-protect"><a href="/yourwiki/index.php?title=Jaz
zMeetDurham&amp;action=protect" title="Protect this page [=]"
accesskey="=">Protect</a></li>
    <li id="ca-delete"><a href="/yourwiki/index.php?title=Jaz
zMeetDurham&amp;action=delete" title="Delete this page [d]"
accesskey="d">Delete</a></li>
    <li id="ca-move"><a href="/yourwiki/index.php/Special:Movepage/
JazzMeetDurham" title="Move this page [m]" accesskey="m">Move</a></li>
    <li id="ca-watch"><a href="/yourwiki/index.php?title=JazzMeetDu
rham&amp;action=watch" title="Add this page to your watchlist [w]"
accesskey="w">Watch</a></li>
    </ul>
    </div>
    </div>
```

Table of Elements: #p-cactions

Element class/id	Purpose
#p-cactions	#p-cactions identifies the containing div for the wiki page's options.
#ca-nstab-main	#ca-nstab-main identifies the list item containing a link to the current wiki page article (as opposed to its discussion page).
#ca-talk	#ca-talk identifies the list item containing a link to the page's talk (discussion) page, if the user is logged in.
#ca-edit	#ca-edit identifies the list item containing a link to edit the current wiki page.
#ca-history	#ca-history identifies the list item containing a link to the history of edits to the page.
#ca-protect	#ca-protect identifies the list item containing a link to protect the page from edits. This is only available if the user is logged in to an administrator account.
#ca-delete	#ca-delete identifies the list item containing a link to delete the current page. This is only available if the user is logged in to an administrator account.
#ca-move	#ca-move identifies the list item of the link to move the page from its current wiki namespace to another. Again, this option is only available if the user is logged in as an administrator.

Element class/id	Purpose
`#ca-watch`	`#ca-watch` identifies the list item containing a link to add the current page to the watchlist of the user's account. This is only available for users who are logged in to an account on your wiki. (This account does not have to be an administrator account.)
`#ca-addsection`	`#ca-addsection` identifies the list item containing the link to add a new section. This is on the discussion (talk) pages.

The JazzMeet design does not display the "Views" header, which indicates the purpose of the links beneath it. So, we can hide it in a way similar to the other headers:

```
#p-navigation h5,
#p-search h5, #p-tb h5, #p-personal h5,
#p-cactions h5 {
display: none !important;
}
```

JazzMeet's design requires that these links are displayed horizontally across the screen. To overcome the character spacing between each list item, a minor change is required to create a negative margin to the right of each list item.

```
#p-cactions ul {
float: right;
list-style-type: none;
}
#p-cactions li {
display: inline;
margin: 0 !important;
padding: 0 !important;
position: relative;
}
#p-cactions li a {
margin: 0 -5px 0 0 !important;
}
```

The links in our JazzMeet design are deep red with a white background, and a red border. If a visitor hovers over the link, we ensure that the underlining disappears to support the idea that they are hovering over a hyperlink.

```
#p-cactions a {
background: #FFFFFF;
border: 1px #8D1425 solid;
color: #8D1425;
padding: 3px;
text-decoration: none;
}
#p-cactions a:hover {
background: #8D1425;
color: #FFFFFF;
}
```

We do not require talk pages on the JazzMeet wiki as the events will be discussed on the event's page. As a result, we can hide the link to the page's talk page. The "watch" feature is also unnecessary for JazzMeet, so we will hide that as well. Because `#ca-addsection` appears only on talk pages, we can hide that as well for good measure.

```
#ca-talk, #ca-watch, #ca-addsection {
display: none;
}
```

`.selected` classifies the list item that is currently selected, to highlight the current view of the visitor. In JazzMeet, the selected option from the page view options needs to be white text with a deep red background.

```
#p-cactions li.selected a {
background: #8C1425 !important;
color: #FFFFFF !important;
}
```

This leaves us with a menu that closely resembles the JazzMeet design's page options. The current view that is being displayed is highlighted with a red background. In this example, it is the "article" view.

The Toolbox: #p-tb

The toolbox, `#p-tb` provides links to useful tools and features relevant to the current page in MediaWiki.

- What links here
- Related changes
- Upload file
- Special pages
- Printable version
- Permanent link

As with most of the divs classified by `.portlet`, the toolbox contains a header indicating the context of the following content, and an unordered list of links for the page, including related changes, a link to the file upload interface, and a link to a printable version of the page.

```
<div class="portlet" id="p-tb">
<h5>Toolbox</h5>
<div class="pBody">
```

```
<ul>
    <li id="t-whatlinkshere"><a href="/yourwiki/index.php/Special:
Whatlinkshere/JazzMeetDurham" title="List of all wiki pages that link
here [j]" accesskey="j">What links here</a></li>
    <li id="t-recentchangeslinked"><a href="/yourwiki/index.php/
Special:Recentchangeslinked/JazzMeetDurham" title="Recent changes in
pages linked from this page [k]" accesskey="k">Related changes</a></
li>
<li id="t-upload"><a href="/yourwiki/index.php/Special:Upload"
title="Upload images or media files [u]" accesskey="u">Upload file</
a></li>
<li id="t-specialpages"><a href="/yourwiki/index.php/
Special:Specialpages" title="List of all special pages [q]"
accesskey="q">Special pages</a></li>
    <li id="t-print"><a href="/yourwiki/index.php?title=JazzMeetDur
ham&amp;printable=yes" title="Printable version of this page [p]"
accesskey="p">Printable version</a></li>
<li id="t-permalink"><a href="/yourwiki/index.php?title=JazzMeetD
urham&amp;oldid=59" title="Permanent link to this version of the
page">Permanent link</a></li>
    </ul>
    </div>
    </div>
```

Table of Elements: #p-tb

Element class/id	Purpose
#p-tb	#p-tb identifies the containing div of the page's toolbox options.
#t-whatlinkshere	#t-whatlinkshere identifies the list item containing a link to a page that displays a list of pages that link to the current page in the wiki.
#t-recentchangeslinked	#t-recentchangeslinked identifies the list item containing a link to a list of pages in the wiki that have recently been changed and are related to the current page in some way.
#t-upload	#t-upload identifies the list item containing a link to the file and image upload interface.
#t-specialpages	#t-specialpages identifies the list item containing a link to a page that lists all "special" pages in your wiki, including the log in interface. A special page is prefixed by "**Special**".

Element class/id	Purpose
#t-print	#t-print identifies the list item containing a link to a printable version of the current page's main content.
#t-permalink	#t-permalink identifies the list item containing a link to the current version of the page.

We will start styling the toolbox by hiding the header in the `<h5>` tag, as we have with the other elements of the wiki.

```
#p-tb h5 {
display: none;
}
```

Next, we need the list of links to be displayed on one line, as in the JazzMeet design, these links are located at the bottom of the page. As most of JazzMeet's visitors will not be looking for these options, we will make the text smaller.

```
#p-tb {
font-size: 70%;
}
#p-tb h5 {
display: none;
}
#p-tb ul {
list-style-type: none;
}
#p-tb li {
display: inline;
}
```

To minimize the focus on these options, we will style the content color and the link color to beige, and ensure that the underline formatting is removed when a visitor hovers over a link.

```
#p-tb, #p-tb a {
color: #857F61;
}
#p-tb a:hover {
text-decoration: none;
}
```

JazzMeet does not require some of the options provided in the toolbox; so they can be hidden.

```
#t-whatlinkshere, #t-permalink, #t-recentchangeslinked {
display: none;
}
```

We are left with a simplified list of options, which will help minimize unnecessary content on the page for the benefit of the wiki's visitor. By removing or hiding them, we lessen the number of options that are dead-ends for the visitor.

Upload file Special pages Printable version

The Search Box: #p-search

The search box in MediaWiki is identified by `#p-search`. The search box contains a header, indicating the purpose of the content below, an input box to accept the visitor's search query, and two buttons. The first of these buttons, **Go**, tries to find a page in the wiki with a title that exactly matches the user's query. If it does not find any, it will display the search results page. The second button, **Search**, displays the search results page regardless of whether the query matches the title of an existing page or not.

```
<div id="p-search" class="portlet">
<h5><label for="searchInput">Search</label></h5>

<div id="searchBody" class="pBody">

<form action="/yourwiki/Special:Search" id="searchform"><div>
<input id="searchInput" name="search" type="text" title="Search
JazzMeet [f]" accesskey="f" value="" />
<input type='submit' name="go" class="searchButton"
id="searchGoButton"     value="Go" /> 
<input type='submit' name="fulltext" class="searchButton" id="mw-
searchButton" value="Search" />
</div>
</form>

</div>
</div>
```

Table of Elements: #p-search

Element class/id	Purpose
#p-search	#p-search identifies the container for the search feature.
#searchInput	#searchInput identifies the input (text) box used to hold the visitor's search query.
#searchGoButton	#searchGoButton identifies an input button of type submit that attempts to find a page with a title matching the "search" query. If an exact match for title is not available, a list of search results for the given search term is displayed.
#mw-searchButton	#mw-searchButton identifies another 'submit' button. This button presents the search results for the search term.

For JazzMeet, we will hide the **Go** and **Search** buttons, because if a visitor presses the return key after entering a query in the search box, the query will be carried out. We could remove the buttons from JazzMeet.php, but it would be useful to leave the buttons in the XHTML, without any styling, for those viewing your wiki.

```
#searchGoButton, #mw-searchButton {
display: none;
}
```

We will also style the search box, #searchInput, with a red border and white background. To make it unique, we will add an icon in the background of the search box, and alter the padding. Altering the padding is necessary because the query string should not cover the search icon when it becomes longer than the width of the input box.

```
#searchInput {
background: #FFFFFF url("searchInput_bg.png") no-repeat center right;
border: 1px #8D1425 solid;
font-size: 80%;
padding: 0;
padding-right: 30px;
width: 165px
}
```

The final result for the search area is a more simplified interface that will be worked in to the new skin's layout in due course.

The Footer: #footer

`#footer` contains the "Powered By MediaWiki" badge, and links to the wiki's privacy policy, disclaimers, the "about" page, information about the number of times the page has been viewed, and the date when it was last modified.

The footer contains an image (the 'Powered By' button) and an unordered list of the links.

```
<div id="footer">

<div id="f-poweredbyico">
<a href="http://www.mediawiki.org/"><img src="/yourwiki/skins/common/
images/poweredby_mediawiki_88x31.png" alt="Powered by MediaWiki" /></
a>
</div>

<ul id="f-list">
<li id="privacy"><a href="/yourwiki/JazzMeet:Privacy_policy"
title="JazzMeet:Privacy policy">Privacy policy</a></li>
<li id="about"><a href="/yourwiki/JazzMeet:About" title="JazzMeet:
About">About JazzMeet</a></li>
<li id="disclaimer"><a href="/yourwiki/JazzMeet:General_disclaimer"
title="JazzMeet:General disclaimer">Disclaimers</a></li>
</ul>

</div>
```

Table of Elements: #footer

There are a few CSS IDs and classes that need to be considered, that appear in the footer area of the website by default.

Element class/id	Purpose
`#footer`	`#footer` identifies the container for the most of your wiki's footer content including the MediaWiki badge, links to your disclaimer, copyright policy, and a page that describes the purpose of the wiki (for example, **About JazzMeet**).
`#f-poweredbyico`	`#f-poweredbyico` identifies a div containing the linked "Powered By MediaWiki" badge.

Element class/id	Purpose
#f-copyrightico	#f-copyrightico identifies a div that contains an image denoting the content licensing type, For example, sGNU. This is not used in MonoBook by default.
#privacy	#privacy identifies the list item containing the link to your wiki's privacy policy.
#about	#about identifies the list item containing the link to a page about your wiki and its purpose – the "about us" page.
#disclaimer	#disclaimer identifies the list item that contains a link to your wiki's disclaimer.

It is wise to keep these pages on your wiki as they provide information to your visitors as to what they can do with the content. It will also make sure that you are not liable for the edits of others.

You can change the appearance of the "Powered By" badge by applying CSS to #f-poweredbyico. To hide it, we can use the following code:

```
#f-poweredbyico {
display: none;
}
```

This method leaves the XHTML in the page. To remove it entirely, you will need to remove the highlighted code below in your skin's PHP template file. Of course, removing it completely means that the visitors do not have to wait for the hidden content to be loaded. This is a good practice for the search engines as well.

```
<?php
if($this->data['poweredbyico']) { ?>
<div id="f-poweredbyico"><?php $this->html('poweredbyico') ?>
</div>
```

If you wish to change the "Powered By MediaWiki" graphic, it is stored as poweredby_mediawiki_88x31.png in the skins/common/images/ directory.

In JazzMeet's design, the "Powered By MediaWiki" badge is replaced by a text that reads "Powered by MediaWiki, from the cool dudes at Wikimedia". To effect this change, we need to delve in to the JazzMeet.php file and change the way in which the footer is generated.

Find the code that relates to the footer's list of links. This will be similar to the code below.

```
<ul id="f-list">
<?php
$footerlinks = array(
'lastmod', 'viewcount', 'numberofwatchingusers', 'credits',
'copyright','privacy', 'about', 'disclaimer', 'tagline',
```

```
);
foreach( $footerlinks as $aLink ) {
if( isset( $this->data[$aLink] ) && $this->data[$aLink] ) {
?>
<li id="<?php echo$aLink?>"><?php $this->html($aLink) ?></li>
<?php }
    }
?>
</ul>
```

The $footerlinks array dynamically inserts the footer links based on the values contained in the array. You can change the URL of the linking pages by changing the content of the pages within your wiki. For example, to change the "about" link in the footer, you can edit the content of MediaWiki:Aboutsite to set the text that is linked, and MediaWiki:Aboutpage to set the link to the relevant page. Similarly, you can edit:

- MediaWiki:Lastmodified to define and display the date on which the page was last modified

- MediaWiki:Privacy to change the link text of the privacy policy link in the footer, and MediaWiki:Privacypage to edit the actual page it links to

- MediaWiki:Viewcount to alter the way the number of page views for the current page is displayed

- MediaWiki:Disclaimers to edit the link text of the link to your disclaimer page, and MediaWiki:Disclaimerpage to edit the link itself

We can remove "credits" (which provides a link to the credits for your wiki), "viewcount" (which displays the number of times the page has been viewed), "numberofwatchingusers" and "tagline" (both of which are unused in MonoBook) as they are not needed in JazzMeet. Now the footer will only contain a link to a page about JazzMeet and a disclaimer.

```
$footerlinks = array(
'about', 'disclaimer',
);
```

numberofwatchingusers

The numberofwatchingusers feature shows the number of visitors watching a particular page in the wiki. It is only shown if $wgPageShowWatchingUsers = true; appears in your LocalSettings.php file.

Now we can add our link to MediaWiki back in to the template file, just before the unordered list closes. In case we want to alter the list item uniquely at a later date, we can assign it the #f-poweredby identifier.

```
<li id="<?php echo$aLink?>"><?php $this->html($aLink) ?></li>
<?php }
    }
?>
<li id="f-poweredby">Powered by <a href="http://www.mediawiki.org/" ti
tle="MediaWiki">MediaWiki</a> from the cool dudes at <a href="http://
www.wikimedia.org/" title="Wikimedia">Wikimedia</a>
</li>
</ul>
```

We can stylize the footer area's content by making the background beige, applying some dark beige borders, and providing adequate padding for the contents of the footer. We can also hide the "Powered By" div, #f-poweredbyico, and the copyright image div, #f-copyrightico.

```
#footer {
background: #D9D5C3;
border-color: #BEB798;
border-style: solid;
border-width: 1px 1px 0 30px;
color: #38230C;
clear: both;
font-family: georgia, "times new roman", times, serif;
font-size: 75%;
line-height: 160%;
padding: 10px 0;
}
#footer ul {
list-style-type: none;
}
#footer li {
display: block;
}
#footer a, #footer a:active, #footer a:link, #footer a:visited {
color: #38230C;
}
#footer a:hover {
text-decoration: none;
}
#f-poweredbyico, #f-copyrightico {
display: none;
}
```

The result looks very similar to our JazzMeet design.

About JazzMeet
Disclaimers
Powered by MediaWiki from the cool dudes at Wikimedia

Summary

In this chapter, we saw how to change the areas surrounding a wiki page's main content, which is classified by `.portlet`. It includes the following:

- Changing the logo of your wiki
- Styling your wiki's navigational elements
- Styling your wiki's userbar elements
- Styling your wiki's page options
- Styling your wiki's toolbox links
- Changing the appearance of the search feature
- Changing your wiki's footer, including adding, and removing links in the PHP template file

The JazzMeet wiki's elements now look the way we want them to, but they are not positioned properly on the page. So in the next chapter, we will learn how to alter the MediaWiki skin's layout.

4
Changing the Layout

In the previous chapters we have seen how to change the wiki's appearance, both within the "article" content, and the areas surrounding it. Currently, the layout is not very attractive, as every element has a full-screen width. This means that the elements you wish to see towards the top of the page, such as your userbar, are displayed towards the bottom of the page. Changing the layout of your MediaWiki skin can overcome this, and will allow you to group the related elements.

In this chapter, we will cover the following:

- Altering your wiki pages' `<head>` element, including changing the default page title, using favicons, and altering stylesheet paths
- Identifying and changing the content block's elements
- Identifying and changing the surrounding interface's elements

Most wikis retain the two-column layout of MonoBook, and our JazzMeet case study is no different. The two columns will allow us to show a smaller column for our "sponsors" alongside the page's main content, without dwarfing the content itself. However, the ordering of content within our PHP template file, `JazzMeet.php`, needs to be changed in order to reflect the use of a right-hand column (as opposed to the left-hand column evident in the MonoBook skin).

Keep Your Head On: MediaWiki's `<head>` Tag

The `<head>` element of the wiki is generated in your skin's PHP template file. In our case, this is `JazzMeet.php`. It contains the wiki page's title, references to the page's stylesheets and, in the case of MonoBook, stylesheets to fix discrepancies in the skin's display in various versions of browsers. Notably, there are fixes for Internet Explorer, Opera, and the KHTML layout engine used by Konqueror and Safari.

The Page Title: <title> and MediaWiki: PageTitle

There are two ways to change the page title of your wiki. The first option is to alter the value contained within the `MediaWiki:Pagetitle` page in your wiki's namespace, to add a slogan after the wiki's name.

```
$1 - JazzMeet - Jazz Festivals
```

Borrow the head content from MonoBook:

If you did not create your PHP template file by copying and renaming the `MonoBook.php` file, you may find it useful to copy this content from another MediaWiki skin template (such as MonoBook), as this will save time.

The second option to change your wiki's page title is to edit the PHP template file in your `skins` directory, changing the value between the `<title>` tags to read:

```
<title>
<?php $this->data['displaytitle']!=""?$this->html('title'):$this->text('title') ?> &bull; JazzMeet
</title>
```

The `highlighted part of the code` retrieves the page article's title. For example, if you have a page in your wiki called **Content**, this command retrieves that value and inserts it in to the `<title>` tag of the page. This changes the page title only for your new skin.

Page Styles: Importing Stylesheets

The following methods can be used to change the stylesheets that your wiki is using:

- Change the skin in your user account preferences (covered in Chapter 1)
- Change the default skin in the `LocalSettings.php` file (also covered in Chapter 1)
- Alter the values in the PHP template file

The first option does not change the stylesheet for all the visitors of your wiki. You should be aware that if you allow the users to change their default skin in their preferences, your wiki could appear "broken" to them. One way to work around this is to force every one of your wiki's visitors to use your skin. You can do this by deleting any file that is not related to your skin in the `skins` directory. Be sure to delete the `SkinName.php` file as well as the associated CSS and image files.

Alternatively, you can specify the skins that MediaWiki is to ignore when presenting a list of available skins to your visitors in their preferences, by adding the names of the skins that should be skipped to `$wgSkinSkins` in `LocalSettings.php`. For example, to remove all of the default skins, simply add the following to your `LocalSettings.php` file:

```
$wgSkipSkins = array("standard", "chick", "cologneblue", "myskin",
"nostalgia", "simple");
```

If you want to specify your wiki's stylesheet by hard-coding it in the template, you can do it by deleting the following:

```
<style type="text/css" media="screen, projection">/*<![CDATA[*/
    @import "<?php $this->text('stylepath') ?>/common/shared.css?<?php
echo $GLOBALS['wgStyleVersion'] ?>";
    @import "<?php $this->text('stylepath') ?>/<?php $this-
>text('stylename') ?>/main.css?<?php echo $GLOBALS['wgStyleVersion']
?>";
/*]]>*/</style>
```

You can replace this with the code below, by wrapping the content of the `<style>` tags in comments. This will prevent older browsers from "seeing" the stylesheet and attempting to apply it to the page.

```
<style type="text/css" media="screen, projection">
<!--@import "skins/jazzmeet/main.css"-->
</style>
```

We will also leave the common print stylesheet stored at `common/commonPrint.css>`, at the top of the page. We will deal with print stylesheets in Chapter 9.

```
<link rel="stylesheet" type="text/css" <?php if(empty($this-
>data['printable']) ) { ?>media="print"<?php } ?> href="<?php $this-
>text('stylepath') ?>/common/commonPrint.css?<?php echo $GLOBALS['wgSt
yleVersion'] ?>" />
```

Content-Type Declaration

Additionally, you can leave the content-type declaration in the header, since this helps your wiki visitor's browser:

```
<meta http-equiv="Content-Type"
content="<?php $this->text('mimetype') ?>; charset=<?php $this-
>text('charset') ?>" />
```

You can hard-code this by replacing the code just mentioned in your skin's PHP template file, with your chosen character set. However, this may be a better option for your wiki, as presenting the wrong charset in a document could cause certain characters to display improperly.

usercss and pagecss

It is not advisable to remove the usercss from the top of the page, because this is used in conjunction with the user's preferences on the wiki. However, if you wish to override them, you can remove them.

For example, if a user has the "justify paragraphs" option set, and the default wiki skin specifies that paragraphs should be right-aligned, the usercss function in the template will insert an inline CSS in to the head of the document to overwrite the right-aligned styling, and present the content as fully justified.

```php
<?php        }
if($this->data['usercss'   ]) { ?>
<style type="text/css">
<?php $this->html('usercss'    ) ?>
</style>
```

The pagecss function inserts page-specific styles into the page, and it can be used to hide things such as the page's main heading, .firstHeading:

```php
<?php if($this->data['pagecss'    ]) { ?>
<style type="text/css">
<?php $this->html('pagecss'    ) ?>
</style>
```

In all likelihood, commenting this out from your template file, or even removing it completely, will not produce any adverse effects to your skin. But it is advisable to leave it in your wiki template's header.

JavaScript: wikibits.js

The wikibits.js file provides useful JavaScript-based enhancements to MediaWiki that are quite probably useful for your wiki, too.

```php
<?php        if($this->data['jsvarurl'  ]) { ?>
<script type="<?php $this->text('jsmimetype') ?>" src="<?php $this->text('jsvarurl'  ) ?>">
<!-- site js -->
</script>
```

Leave both the wikibits.js (stored in common) and site.js files linked in the header. wikibits.js aids wiki-related elements such as the table of contents and the "diff" interface.

Favicon: favicon.ico

A favicon is a small graphic that appears in the left of your Internet browser's address bar. Favicons can help your wiki to be more easily recognized in the bookmark lists of your visitor's browser, and in the tabs of certain browsers.

The favicon in MediaWiki can be changed in two ways. Firstly, you can upload an icon image file, `favicon.ico`, to your wiki's root directory. Secondly, you can edit the `$wgFavicon` setting in the `LocalSettings.php` file to `$wgScriptPath/path/to/your/favicon.ico`, as follows:

```
$wgFavicon = "$wgScriptPath/skins/jazzmeet/favicon.ico"
```

`$wgScriptPath` is your wiki's "base" – the root of your wiki's installation.

> Ensure that the entire name of your `favicon.ico` file is in lowercase characters. Some servers, such as those running on UNIX-based operating systems, will not display the icon unless its name is completely written in lowercase.

Changing the Content Area: #bodyContent

If you study the XHTML output from the MonoBook theme, you will notice that the page's primary content is positioned above the "interface" elements such as the userbar, page navigation, and the logo. This helps to improve the meaning of the page's content.

Page Anchors

Towards the top of the document, you will see `<a name="top" id="top"></a>` as an anchor, identified by `#top`. This allows you to include a "back to the top of this page" link within your wiki's design. This is unused in MediaWiki's MonoBook skin, but we can use it for the JazzMeet skin by inserting a link in our template just above the `</div>` of `#bodyContent` (the added code is highlighted):

```
<!-- start content -->
<?php $this->html('bodytext') ?>
    <?php if($this->data['catlinks']) { ?><div id="catlinks"><?php
$this->html('catlinks') ?></div><?php } ?>
<p id="f-top">
    <a href="#top" title="Return to the top of this page">Top of this
page</a>
```

```
</p>
<!-- end content -->
<div class="visualClear"></div>
</div>
```

We assigned the paragraph an identity, #f-top, to make it easier to style in the future, if needed. There are more page anchors in the jump-to section.

Headings

Inside #content, the wiki page's content area, there are two headings: the page title (.firstHeading) and your wiki's "tagline" (#siteSub).

The page title, .firstHeading, is contained within a <h1> tag, as the primary title for the content:

```
<h1 class="firstHeading">
<?php $this->data['displaytitle']!=""?$this->html('title'):$this-
>text('title') ?>
</h1>
```

The highlighted PHP retrieves the page's title, and inserts it in the <h1> heading tags. The tagline is in a level-3 heading (<h3>), and will insert "From JazzMeet" to the page, just beneath the page title. This will give an indication of where the content came from. Although we have hidden it using CSS in the JazzMeet skin, we can remove it from the page in the following manner:

```
<h3 id="siteSub">
<?php $this->msg('tagline') ?>
</h3>
```

Alternatively, you can change the tagline that appears in your wiki's new skin by hard-coding it, as follows:

```
<h3 id="siteSub">Courtesy of JazzMeet</h3>
```

The remaining headings within the content area are already styled as desired for JazzMeet.

Content Blocks

Despite representing the majority of the pages' content in your wiki, the content block has perhaps the simplest code in the PHP template file for your skin.

contentSub

The #contentSub divs contain messages that are not frequently needed, such as the page title of the redirecting template:

```
<div id="contentSub"><?php $this->html('subtitle') ?></div>
<?php if($this->data['undelete']) { ?><div id="contentSub2"><?php
  $this->html('undelete') ?></div><?php } ?>
```

As with most elements in the wiki's main content block, these may look useless to you, but beware of removing them. The deletion of #contentSub makes it difficult for an average wiki user to return to the page that he or she was redirected from (for example, to remove the redirect).

"New Talk"

The new talk block in the template inserts a note in the page, if your wiki's user has a new message on their talk page (that is, a change has been made to User_Talk: VisitorsUserName). This is displayed for both visitors who are logged in to an account on your wiki, and anonymous visitors (whose username is their Internet Protocol address).

```
<?php if($this->data['newtalk'] ) { ?><div class="usermessage"><?php
$this->html('newtalk')   ?></div><?php }
```

Unless you want your wiki's users to be notified of the new messages on their talk page, it is wise to leave this block in the PHP template file. Removing it could just alienate your wiki's visitors.

Jump-To Links

The jump-to links in MediaWiki's template are inserted by the following code:

```
<?php if($this->data['showjumplinks']) { ?><div id="jump-to-
nav"><?php $this->msg('jumpto') ?> <a href="#column-one"><?php $this-
>msg('jumptonavigation') ?></a>, <a href="#searchInput"><?php $this-
>msg('jumptosearch') ?></a></div><?php } ?>
```

These provide links to the anchors in the page, such as the navigation and the search feature. JazzMeet's skin hides them, but we want them to remain in the template file to make the navigation around the page easier, for any visitors using screenreaders.

Page Content

Your wiki's primary content can be retrieved using the following PHP call:

```php
<?php $this->html('bodytext') ?>
```

It is advisable to insert your wiki page's content **once** per page. If there is anything more, it would (quite rightly) be seen as "spam" by the search engines, because it is unnecessary to repeat your wiki's content multiple times in a page.

Category Links

Category links can be inserted into the wiki's page using the `[[Category:Category Name]]` syntax. Traditionally left towards the bottom of the content, they provide a useful way for the visitors to find pages of a similar topic on your wiki. Assigning categories to pages also generates lists of all of the pages contained within the category. You can insert category links in the following way:

```php
<?php if($this->data['catlinks']) { ?>
<div id="catlinks"><?php $this->html('catlinks') ?></div><?php } ?>
```

For JazzMeet, we will leave the category links at the bottom of the page. They have already been styled to have a smaller text size using CSS to minimize their space on each page.

Changing the Interface

As demonstrated with the interface elements in Chapter 3, you can add and remove elements directly from the interface. You can move the content blocks and elements around, too, to create a different layout.

The editinterface permission:

The "editinterface" permission needs to be enabled by you to edit the interface elements through MediaWiki pages. By default, users having administrator privileges are able to edit these pages.

MediaWiki Interface Element Pages

In MediaWiki 1.5 and above, you can change your wiki's navigation, and a host of other interface elements' content. You can do this without having to sift through PHP, by editing the content of certain pages in your wiki's namespace.

Wiki Navigation: MediaWiki:Sidebar

The `MediaWiki:Sidebar` page in your wiki controls the navigation links. The wiki-syntax for editing this page is as follows:

```
* Heading
** Wiki URL of page|Link text
* Another heading
** Another wiki URL|More link text
```

The navigation element in the JazzMeet design was just hidden, and not removed. By inserting some wiki markup to this page, we can create a useful menu for those who may be using screenreaders to navigate to some specific parts of the wiki.

> **Blank interface pages:**
>
> You can prevent anything from being displayed in the interface by editing the relevant MediaWiki interface pages to read (that is, a single hyphen). So, if the `MediaWiki:Sidebar` page contained just a single hyphen, the navigation links would not appear at all.

```
* Jazz Festivals in
** category:JazzMeetUK|UK
** category:JazzMeetEurope|Europe
** category:JazzMeetAmerica|America
** category:JazzMeetAsia|Asia
** category:JazzMeetAfrica|Africa
```

This generates a list of hyperlinks to the indicate pages, with the provided link text. Note that each link is uniquely identified with an id of the linked page's name, and "n- prefix" as the snippet of XHTML. Refer to the following code:

```
<h5>Jazz Festivals in</h5>
<div class='pBody'>
<ul>
    <li id="n-Category:JazzMeetUK"><a href="index.php/Category:
JazzMeetUK">Category:JazzMeetUK</a></li>
    <li id="n-Category:JazzMeetEurope"><a href="index.php/Category:
JazzMeetEurope">Category:JazzMeetEurope</a></li>
    <li id="n-Category:JazzMeetAmerica"><a href="index.php/Category:
JazzMeetAmerica">Category:JazzMeetAmerica</a></li>
    <li id="n-Category:JazzMeetAsia"><a href="index.php/Category:
JazzMeetAsia">Category:JazzMeetAsia</a></li>
    <li id="n-Category:JazzMeetAfrica"><a href="index.php/Category:
JazzMeetAfrica">Category:JazzMeetAfrica</a></li>
</ul>
</div>
```

The unstyled list will look similar to the following screenshot (assuming there is no CSS hiding it):

Jazz Festivals in

- Category:JazzMeetUK
- Category:JazzMeetEurope
- Category:JazzMeetAmerica
- Category:JazzMeetAsia
- Category:JazzMeetAfrica

We need to style it to match JazzMeet's appearance. For this , we will give the area a deep red background and a curved red corner in the top-left corner, as in the concept for the design, using:

```
#p-Jazz_Festivals_in {
background: #8C1425 url("p-jazz_festivals_in_bg.png") no-repeat top
left;
color: #FFFFFF;
font-size: 70%;
padding: 5px;
}
    #p-Jazz_Festivals_in h5 {
    color: #FFFFFF;
    display: inline;
    font-weight: normal;
    }
```

We will give the links in the list a white colored text, remove the bottom border when the links are hovered over by a visitor, and ensure that the list is displayed on a single line. Refer to the following code:

```
#p-Jazz_Festivals_in a {
border-color: #FFFFFF;
color: #FFFFFF;
}
#p-Jazz_Festivals_in a:hover {
border-bottom-width: 0;
}
#p-Jazz_Festivals_in ul {
display: inline;
list-style-type: none;
margin: 0;
}
#p-Jazz_Festivals_in li {
display: inline;
margin: 0 5px 0 0;
}
```

The navigation now looks similar to the one in JazzMeet's concept.

MediaWiki:Sitenotice

You can insert a site-wide notice in to your wiki's pages by editing the content of the `MediaWiki:Sitenotice` page. For example, changing this page's wiki markup to "`This is a site notice - [[JazzMeetDurham]]`" will result in the following message being displayed above the page's main title:

> This is a site notice - JazzMeetDurham
>
> ◉ **MediaWiki:Main**

The "Special" Page Tab

You can remove the "special" page tab (that appears on the log in page) by editing the `includes/SkinTemplate.php` file, and commenting out (or removing) the code for this as follows:

```
/*
$content_actions['article'] = array(
'class' => 'selected',
'text' => wfMsg('specialpage'),
'href' => $wgRequest->getRequestURL()
);
*/
```

This hides the "special" tab for all skins that have been enabled for your wiki.

MediaWiki: MenuNavigation

Your wiki's navigation is, by default, generated in your skin's template file. But you can allow administrators on your wiki to change your wiki's navigation by editing the `MediaWiki:MenuNavigation` page's content:

```
<h5><?php $out = wfMsg( $bar ); if (wfNoMsg($bar, $out)) echo $bar;
else echo $out; ?></h5>
<div class='pBody'>
<ul>
```

```
<?php foreach($cont as $key => $val) { ?>
<li id="<?php echo htmlspecialchars($val['id']) ?>">
<a href="<?php echo htmlspecialchars($val['href']) ?>">
<?php echo htmlspecialchars($val['text'])?></a></li>
<?php } ?>
</ul>
</div>
```

By replacing the highlighted code in your skin's PHP template file with `<?php $this->msgWiki( 'MenuNavigation' ) ?>`, you can add navigation to your wiki by editing the `MediaWiki:MenuNavigation` page.

The Edit Toolbar

The edit interface's toolbar allows your wiki's visitors to format a page's content with minimal knowledge of wiki markup. It provides buttons to create links, make the selected text bold or italic, and insert mathematical formulae and images.

Toolbar buttons

You can add to or remove options from the edit toolbar with relative ease in the `EditPage.php` file that is in the `includes` directory of your wiki's installation path. Find the `getEditToolbar()` function in this file, and you will notice a number of arrays, each defining a single button in the toolbar. As an example, we will consider the internal link button:

```
array(    'image'      => 'button_link.png',
          'id'         => 'mw-editbutton-link',
          'open'       => '[[',
          'close'      => ']]',
          'sample'=> wfMsg('link_sample'),
          'tip'        => wfMsg('link_tip'),
          'key'        => 'L'
     )
```

The first line defines the image to be used for the button. This is stored in `skins/common/images/`. The second line assigns an id to the toolbar button, so it can be uniquely identified. The next two lines, open and close, define the opening and closing of the wiki markup for the function in question. In this case, `[[`' opens a `link to another wiki page, whilst '[[`' closes the link. The context within these brackets become the linked text.

The `sample` and `tip` parameters provide references to the MediaWiki interface pages that can be edited to provide an explanatory text for your button.

The page `MediaWiki:link_sample`, defined by the value `sample` in the array, provides an example of the wiki mark-up inserted between the `open` and `close` parameters specified above it. In this case, this contains '**Link title**', as this is the content of the `MediaWiki:link_sample` page:

MediaWiki:Link sample
Link title

Inserted between the open and close values, this would create a link in wiki mark-up:

```
[[Link title]]
```

The value of `tip` provides a reference to the `MediaWiki:link_tip` page, where you can create a brief description of what it is the button does. Since this button creates an internal link (i.e., a link to another page within your wiki), its content is '**Internal link**'.

MediaWiki:Link tip
Internal link

Adding a new toolbar button

Because JazzMeet is about people interacting and creating jazz festivals, there will probably be a lot of links to user profiles on the wiki. So, we can add a new "user page link" button to the edit interface's toolbar as follows:

```
array(     'image'     => 'button_user-link.png',
           'id'        => 'mw-editbutton-userlink',
           'open'      => '[[User:',
           'close'     => ']]',
        'sample'=> wfMsg('user-link_sample'),
        'tip' => wfMsg('user-link_tip'),
        'key' => 'U'
    )
```

The order of the arrays affects the order in which the buttons appear in the toolbar. We will insert our new button at the end of the toolbar, beneath the arrays for other buttons in the `EditPage.php` file.

The button images are 23 by 22 pixels in dimension, by default. We can upload a new button image to the `skins/common /images/` directory. We will also need to add the sample and tip text. The sample text should be added to `MediaWiki: User-link_sample`:

    User:Richard

 This text is inserted between the opening and closing markup tags of MediaWiki that have been specified in the array. In this case, they are "[[' and ']]" respectively.

`MediaWiki:User-link_tip` can then be edited to provide some help as to what the button does, and whether a visitor should hover the cursor over it.

    Link to a user's page.

The result should be the addition of the "user-link" button to the end of the toolbar buttons, visible in the edit and the preview interfaces of your wiki.

Creating Your Own Template

Now that we have discussed the various blocks and elements in your skin's template file, we can change the layout of the wiki's new skin.

You can use your own classes and ids in your template, but it is better to use MediaWiki's default names for them, because:

- If others edit your skin's template file or CSS, it will make it easier for them to work out what's going on, if they are familiar with MediaWiki.
- Some class and id names (for example, the navigation list items) are automatically generated by MediaWiki, by default.
- It is more consistent, as the other skins for your wiki are presented with those names. As a result, it is easier to make cross-skin changes.

Ordering Elements

As we have used the MonoBook template as the basis for our new skin, the ordering of the elements within the page is not quite right for our JazzMeet skin's layout. In MonoBook, the ordering within the body is as follows:

- The page's primary content:
    - Page title
    - Your wiki's tagline
    - "New message" notification, if needed
    - `jump-to-nav` links, to skip to either the wiki's navigation or the search feature
    - The content itself
    - The category links, if any
    - The print footer

- The interface:
    - Views (for example, edit page, view page history)
    - Personal tools (for example, log in, log out, preferences)
    - The logo
    - Navigation
    - Search
    - Toolbox
    - The wiki's footer

The following order needs to be adopted to produce the layout required for JazzMeet:

- The page's header, which contains the wiki's logo and the personal tools element
- The column content, including links to JazzMeet's sponsors, and the search feature
- The views and navigation elements
- The page's primary content (this remains the same as mentioned earlier)
    - Page title
    - Your wiki's tagline
    - "New message" notification, if needed
    - `jump-to-nav` links, to skip to either the wiki's navigation or the search feature
    - The content itself
    - The category links, if any
    - The print footer

- The toolbox
- The footer

Content Ordering

Ideally, we want each page's primary content to be as close to the top of the page as possible. This is not only good for the search engines, as they can instantly see what your page is about, but is also better for those who use text-only Internet browsers.

Layouts with CSS

To create the basic two-column layout that is required for JazzMeet's design, we can use the following:

```
<div id="globalWrapper">
<div id="content">
<!-- main content here -->
</div>
<div id="column-one">
<!-- column content here -->
</div>
<div style="clear: both !important;"></div>
</div>
```

By assigning widths to the content and the column divs and making them float left, we can easily create a two-column layout that positions the primary content higher in the page's structure than the content in the column. Thus, the CSS would be as follows:

```
#globalWrapper {
margin: 0 auto; /* centre the layout */
width: 950px;
}
#content {
float: left;
width: 710px;
}
#column-one {
float: left;
width: 215px;
}
```

More CSS-based Layouts:

There are a lot of CSS resources on the Internet. Two of the best are **Bluerobot's Layout Reservoir** (http://www.bluerobot. com/web/layouts/), and **Position is Everything** (http://www. positioniseverything.net/).

Moving Blocks Around

Currently, the JazzMeet wiki's content is in a single column, with the page's primary content displayed above other elements such as the toolbox and navigation links, and the search feature.

Back up your skin template frequently:

Moving the content around in the template can become messy. So make sure you create copies of your skin template frequently, just in case!

JazzMeet's design means that we will need two columns, with the primary content to the left, and the other content, such as the search feature and our sponsors to the right, as we demonstrated earlier.

The Header

We have already dealt with the `<head>` elements. First in the page's `<body>` are the `#p-personal` element and the wiki's logo, which we need to enclose in a new div to style them more effectively. We can insert the following existing div inside:

```
<div id="header">

<div class="portlet" id="p-personal">
<h5><?php $this->msg('personaltools') ?></h5>
<div class="pBody">
<ul>
<?php foreach($this->data['personal_urls'] as $key => $item) { ?>
    <li id="pt-<?php echo Sanitizer::escapeId($key) ?>"<?php
if ($item['active']) { ?> class="active"<?php } ?>><a href="<?php
        echo htmlspecialchars($item['href']) ?>"<?php echo $skin-
>tooltipAndAccesskey('pt-'.$key) ?><?php
if(!empty($item['class'])) { ?> class="<?php
        echo htmlspecialchars($item['class']) ?>"<?php } ?>><?php
        echo htmlspecialchars($item['text']) ?></a></li>
<?php} ?>
</ul>
```

```
    </div>
    </div>
    <img src="jazzmeet_logo.png" alt="JazzMeet logo" />
    </div><!--end header-->
```

To correctly display the above div, we need to specify some style rules:

```
#header {
background: #FFFFFF url("header_bg.png") no-repeat top right;
height: 85px;
}
    #header img {
    float: left;
}
```

`#globalWrapper` needs a little styling in order to create a fixed width design, and to use a background color for the right-hand column in accordance with our JazzMeet design. The height of the page content does not matter.Refer to the following code:

```
#globalWrapper {
background: #D9D5C3;
margin: 0 auto;
padding: 0;
width: 950px;
}
```

The `#content` area needs a defined width, and has to float to the left, alongside the column to its right:

```
#content {
background: #E6E4D8 url("content_bg.gif") repeat-y top left;
color: #000000;
float: left;
font-family: georgia, "times new roman", times, serif;
padding: 0px 5px 10px 35px;
width: 710px;
}
```

As we have inserted the JazzMeet logo in the header, we can remove the PHP that generates it further down the skin. This code is identified as follows:

```
<div class="portlet" id="p-logo">
<a style="background-image: url(skins/common/images/wiki.png);"
href="index.php/Main_Page" title="Visit the Main Page [z]"
accesskey="z"></a>
</div>
<script type="text/javascript"> if (window.isMSIE55) fixalpha();
</script>
```

The Content Column: #column-one

The JazzMeet design has a column along the right-hand side of the page's primary content that displays JazzMeet's sponsors, and some advertisements. In the order of our page for JazzMeet, this content comes before the page's primary content.

Beneath the closing tag for our new header, we can now add the necessary content for our column that includes the search feature:

```
<div id="column-one">

<div id="p-search" class="portlet">
<h5><label for="searchInput"><?php $this->msg('search') ?></label>
</h5>
<div id="searchBody" class="pBody">
<form action="<?php $this->text('searchaction') ?>"
id="searchform"><div>
<input id="searchInput" name="search" type="text"<?php echo $skin->too
ltipAndAccesskey('search');
if( isset( $this->data['search'] ) ) {
    ?> value="<?php $this->text('search') ?>"<?php } ?> />
<input type='submit' name="go" class="searchButton"
id="searchGoButton" value="<?php $this->msg('searcharticle') ?>"
/> 
<input type='submit' name="fulltext" class="searchButton" id="mw-
searchButton" value="<?php $this->msg('searchbutton') ?>" />
</div>
</form>
</div>
</div>

</div><!-- end column-one-->
```

Above the closing tag for the `#column-one` div, we can include our sponsor's logos, as well as a header in preparation for the advertisements that will be displayed:

```
<h5 class="sponsors"><span>Sponsors</span></h5>
<img src="wiki-install-path/sponsor_packt.png" alt="Sponsor: Packt" />
<img src="wiki-install-path/sponsor_peacock-carter.png" alt="Sponsor:
Peacock Carter" />

<h5 class="advertisements"><span>Advertisements</span></h5>

</div><!-- end column-one-->
```

These images need styling, because we have previously styled images in the content area:

```
#column-one img {
border: 2px #BEB798 solid;
margin: 7px;
}
```

We also need to replace the header's text with an image of the text, because most people will not have Hick Design's "Hill House", the font used in the JazzMeet logo:

```
h5.sponsors, h5.advertisements {
height: 21px;
border-bottom: 1px #BEB798 solid;
border-top: 1px #BEB798 solid;
width: 195px;
}
h5.sponsors {
background: transparent url("h5_sponsor.png") no-repeat top left;
}
h5.advertisements {
background: transparent url("h5_advertisement.png") no-repeat top
left;
}
h5.sponsors span, h5.advertisements span {
display: none !important;
}
```

The above-mentioned technique is useful for displaying headings and small amounts of text in a font that many of your visitors may not have. But beware that its overuse could result in search engine penalties. The best practice is to use this technique sparingly, and replicate the exact text within the heading in the image that is replacing it.

The Content Body

We need to make changes to the content body's order, such as the wiki's navigation, that appears above the `#content` div, inside `#column-content`. Because we have defined these links in `MediaWiki:Sidebar`, we need to have them inserted in to the template dynamically:

```
<div id="column-content">

<div class='portlet' id='p-<?php echo Sanitizer::escapeId($bar)
?>'<?php echo $skin->tooltip('p-'.$bar) ?>>
<h5>
<?php $out = wfMsg( $bar ); if (wfEmptyMsg($bar, $out)) echo $bar;
else echo $out; ?>
</h5>
<div class='pBody'>
<ul>
<?php foreach($cont as $key => $val) { ?>
<li id="<?php echo Sanitizer::escapeId($val['id']) ?>"<?php
if ( $val['active'] ) { ?> class="active" <?php }?>>
```

```
<a href="<?php echo htmlspecialchars($val['href']) ?>"<?php echo
$skin->tooltipAndAccesskey($val['id']) ?>><?php echo htmlspecialchars(
$val['text']) ?></a></li>
<?php        } ?>
</ul>
</div>
</div>
<?php } ?>

<div id="content">
```

The toolbox in the PHP template file (look for `<div class="portlet" id="p-tb">`) should be moved to just above the closing tag for #bodyContent, in order to insert it at the bottom of the primary content area. In the next few chapters, we will learn how to insert social-bookmarking links and a printable stylesheet for MediaWiki.

The Footer

The footer for the JazzMeet skin is located just outside the #content div. Refer to the following code:

```
</div><!-- end content-->
<div id="footer">
<ul id="f-list">
<?php
        $footerlinks = array(
        'about', 'disclaimer',
);
        foreach( $footerlinks as $aLink ) {
            if( isset( $this->data[$aLink] ) && $this->data[$aLink] ) {
?>
    <li id="<?php echo$aLink?>"><?php $this->html($aLink) ?></li>
<?php }
}
?>
<li id="f-poweredby">Powered by <a href="http://www.mediawiki.org/" ti
tle="MediaWiki">MediaWiki</a> from the cool dudes at <a href="http://
www.wikimedia.org/" title="Wikimedia">Wikimedia</a></li>
<li id="f-top"><a href="#top" title="Return to the top of this
page">Top of this page</a></li>
</ul>
</div>
```

This dynamically inserts links to the "about" and "disclaimers" pages of our wiki, and statically inserts a link back to MediaWiki and Wikimedia.

End Of The Template File

Be sure to include the code `<script type="text/javascript">if (window.runOnloadHook) runOnloadHook();</script>` just above the `</body>` tag in your template file. Some of the functions in MediaWiki rely on it. You will also need to restore warnings (`wfRestoreWarnings()`) in the PHP file, once your template has been created:

```php
<?php $this->html('bottomscripts'); /* JS call to runBodyOnloadHook */
?>
</div>
<?php $this->html('reporttime') ?>
<script type="text/javascript">if (window.runOnloadHook)
runOnloadHook();</script>
</body>
</html>
<?php
    wfRestoreWarnings();
} // end of execute() method
} // end of class
?>
```

`<?php $this->html('reporttime') ?>` creates commented text at the bottom of your wiki's page.

The Result

The resulting pages, and the associated style and images generated with the template, resemble our vision for JazzMeet a lot more closely.

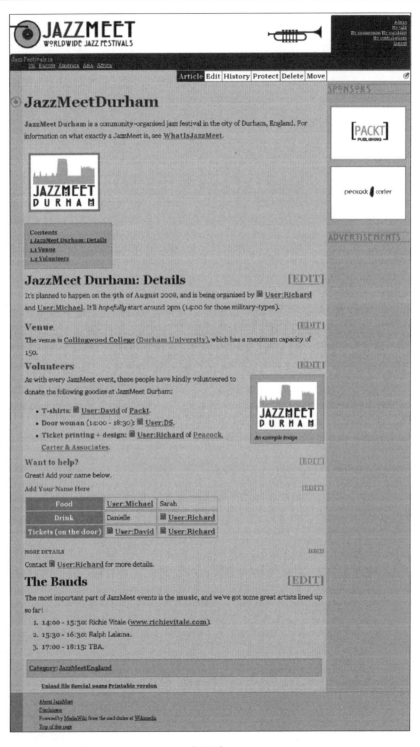

Summary

In this chapter, we discussed how to change the layout of your MediaWiki skin, as well as the possible alterations that can be made to the `<head>` element of the wiki's template. Thus, we have covered the following:

- The elements of the wiki's `<head>` block, and their characteristics
- The elements of the wiki's content block, and their characteristics
- The elements of the wiki's interface, their characteristics, and the ways in which we can add additional buttons to the edit interface's toolbar
- Creating your new skin's PHP template file, by merging the elements from an existing skin in to your skin's XHTML file

Useful MediaWiki Functions

5

A MediaWiki skin template file, which is similar to `JazzMeet.php`, is a mixture of PHP and XHTML, with a smattering of JavaScript and inline CSS as well. There are a significant number of useful PHP-based MediaWiki functions that can be used (in some cases, re-used) to modify your wiki's skin. In this chapter, we will discuss the following:

- The basics of how to use MediaWiki functions in your skin
- Useful functions for your wiki's `<head>` section
- Functions for your wiki's content area
- Functions for your wiki's interface area

PHP Functions and MediaWiki Functions

PHP functions are built-in functions of the PHP language. For example, the `str_replace` function allows you to replace one substring with another, within a string.

MediaWiki functions extend the PHP functions in a way that is helpful for your MediaWiki wiki. Some of these are in the `SkinTemplate.php` file in the `includes` directory, and there are yet more functions in the `Skins.php` file in the same directory.

Using MediaWiki Functions

To get data from MediaWiki to your page, there are two steps:

- Retrieving the data, via a function or a variable
- Formatting the data in a suitable format

Retrieving the Data

Before we can do anything with the information, we need to retrieve it, be it from a variable, or from a function.

Retrieving Data from a Variable

To retrieve data from a variable, you can just call it in your skin template. For example, to retrieve the data within the variable "var" from the object "Object", all you need to do is this:

```
$Object['var']
```

Although this retrieves the value that the variable is holding, it does not output (that is display) the variable. To do this, we use PHP's echo language constraint (a sort of function):

```
<?php echo $Object['var'] ?>
```

 The variables you can access in your skin template are prefixed with "$tpl" in the SkinTemplate.php file.

Retrieving Data from a Function

In a similar way, we can retrieve data from a function to use it in our skin template. Using the function getData(), we will retrieve the data stored within the "var" variable from "Object":

```
$Object -> getData('var')
```

Again, we need to output this using echo:

```
<?php echo $Object -> getData('var') ?>
```

Now that we have the data, it is simply a matter of ensuring that it is formatted to suit our needs.

Formatting the Data

Once you have accessed the information you need from MediaWiki functions, it may need to be converted in to a suitable format for output. For example, if the function or variable that used to give you data returned a URL you would probably need to ensure that the URL was properly 'escaped' (so 'and' becomes '&', and so on). The following are some useful transformations:

- html
- htmlentities

- htmlspecialchars
- text
- urlencode

html

html is particular to MediaWiki, and acts in a similar way to text.

htmlentities

htmlentities() is used to escape all characters that have HTML equivalents. To decode data in htmlentities format, you can use the html_entity_decode() function.

htmlspecialchars

You can use htmlspecialchars() to escape just a few of the following characters, which are most likely to cause problems in XHTML: the ampersand, double quote, single quote, and the less than and greater than characters.

text

Perhaps not surprisingly, you can use text() (again, particular to MediaWiki) to insert the retrieved information in your skin template. This function simply returns the unaltered variable or value with no changes.

Let's suppose that we want to insert the page title elsewhere in our MediaWiki skin template. To retrieve it, we need to retrieve the data from $this, and format its output as a text within a paragraph:

```
<p>
<?php echo $this->text('title') ?>
</p>
```

We will have a look at some examples of both the retrieval and formatting of variables.

Functions for <head>

We covered the basics of the <head> element in your MediaWiki skin template in the previous chapter, but we can still make some changes in the head of the wiki template.

Headlinks

`<?php $this->html('headlinks') ?>` retrieves links to favicons for use with MediaWiki (as specified by the `$wgFavicon` variable in the `LocalSettings.php` file), and also provides a reference to your wiki's Open Search Description. It thus produces XHTML code similar to the following:

```
<link rel="shortcut icon" href="/favicon.ico" />
<link rel="search" type="application/opensearchdescription+xml"
href="/richard.carter/book/v1/opensearch_desc.php" title="JazzMeet
(English)" />
```

This function also inserts related keywords in the `<head>` of the page, based on the title of the page, and the internal links within the page's content.

Pagetitle

The wiki's current page title can be inserted in the page using the `<?php $this->text('pagetitle') ?>` function. Notice that the formatting of this data is `text`, as opposed to anything else, as it is used directly in the page as content.

Most MediaWiki skins use this only once: within the `<title>` tags, and again in the content block, in the `<h1>` element. But `.firstHeading` may benefit your wiki's visitors to insert the page title again. For example, you may wish to include the page's title in a link to a social bookmarking website such as Digg:

```
<a href="http://www.digg.com/submit?url=http://www.example.
com&amp;title= <?php $this->html('pagetitle') ?>" title="Add this page
to Digg!">
Add this page, <?php $this->text('pagetitle') ?>, to Digg!
</a>
```

The formatting of the first instance is `html`, because the page title is being used within a link.

ServerURL

`serverurl` returns the URL of the server on which MediaWiki is installed. This is generally the domain of your website, for example `http://www.example.com`. For most uses, this should be encoded using `urlencode`.

```
<?php $this->urlencode('serverurl') ?>
```

Skinname

`skinname` is the variable holding the current MediaWiki skin's name. In the case of JazzMeet, it would return `jazzmeet`. For example, if you want to specify the stylesheet on your own, you can insert the following into your skin template:

```
<style type="text/css" media="screen, projection">
<!--
@import "skins/<?php $this->text('skinname') ?>/main.css"
-->
</style>
```

 The value of this variable is set at the top of your skin's PHP template file, in a line similar to this: `$this->skinname = 'jazzmeet'`

Stylepath

`<?php $this->text('stylepath') ?>` returns the directory used by your installation of MediaWiki to refer to its skins. By default, this is `/skins/common/shared.css` and the location of the current skin's stylesheet is `/skins/jazzmeet/main.css`, for JazzMeet.

 The Style Path:

The variable returned here can be specified in the `LocalSettings.php` file. It is called as `$wgStylePath`.

Stylename

`stylename` holds the value of your skin's style name. It is generally similar to the value of `skinname`.

StyleVersion

`<?php echo $GLOBALS['wgStyleVersion'] ?>` adds the current version of the style (an integer) to the page, and in the MonoBook theme, it is added after the specified stylesheet's path.

TrackbackHTML

The PHP `if ($this->data['trackbackhtml']) print $this->>data['trackbackhtml']; ?>` inserts trackback links in to the head of your wiki's page.

Trackback links provide a way of requesting notification when someone links to a page on your wiki. For more information, refer to the Wikipedia's article on Trackbacks at: http://en.wikipedia.org/wiki/Trackback.

UserCSS

usercss holds any additional style that has been requested by the user, and needs to be nested within <style> tags, for example, formatting paragraphs' alignment to be justified.

```
<style type="text/css">
<?php $this->html('usercss'   ) ?>
</style>
```

Functions For <body>

The body of your wiki can be split in two distinct areas: First is the content area, which contains the majority of the page's content, including that page's editable content within MediaWiki. Second is the interface area, which includes menu links, your wiki's logo, and the footer.

Within <body>

Two JavaScript events, "inserted if" and "when required"' and a unique class for the page are inserted in to the <body> tag of each page in MediaWiki. A typical page's <body> tag looks similar to the following code. Note the absence of the JavaScript events:

```
<body class="mediawiki ns-0 ltr page-Main_Page">
```

The JavaScript events provide for double-clicking events, and the page load event. They are required on the page being generated by the PHP template:

```
<?php if($this->data['body_ondblclick']) { ?>ondblclick="<?php $this-
>text('body_ondblclick') ?>"<?php } ?>

<?php if($this->data['body_onload'   ]) { ?>onload="<?php    $this-
>text('body_onload')     ?>"<?php } ?>
```

The page class insertion consists of a number of functions. Within the class"" assignment, .dir returns the direction of the wiki's content (either ltr or rtl, left-to-right and right-to-left, respectively) .pageclass inserts the remainder of the

page's class in the page, based on the current page's title, in the format
page-Page_Title, where Page_Title is the title of the current wiki page.

```
<body class="<?php $this->text('nsclass') ?> <?php $this->text('dir')
?> <?php $this->text('pageclass') ?>">
```

> **Spacing between class names:**
> Note the spacing between the functions that return the class names for
> a page. Without spacing, the page will not be assigned the multiple
> classes that are intended, but one class, which is a concatenation of all of
> your intended classes.

Functions for page content

In MediaWiki, the page content has a number of functions associated with it,
including those for inserting:

- The "sitenotice", a globally-displayed notice controlled by the wiki's
  administrators.

- The subtitle of your wiki into the page: This is the name of your wiki,
  prefixed with the word "from". For example, in Wikipedia, this is
  "From Wikipedia".

- A notification if a user has a new message on his/her talk page

- The internal page navigation links, to skip to the other areas of the page, for
  example, the top or the search box.

- The page's user-contributed content, the "bodycontent".

ArticleID

articleid holds the value of the current article's unique identification number,
which is used in keeping track of your articles' versions. Generally, we would want
to retrieve this data as text:

```
<?php $this->text('articleid') ?>
```

Bodytext

The wiki page's main content, the "bodytext"', is inserted with this simple command:
`<?php $this->html('bodytext') ?>`. This inserts the formatted XHTML that
constitutes the content of the page.

Category Links

The category links associated with each page are inserted in a conditional statement:

```php
<?php if($this->data['catlinks']) { ?>
<div id="catlinks">
<?php        $this->html('catlinks') ?>
</div>
<?php } ?>
```

Traditionally in MediaWiki, the category links are inserted directly below the primary content. This makes sense, because providing a way for your visitors to find related information under the article or page that they just read will keep your wiki's visitor reading the content on your wiki.

Jump to navigation links

The `#jump-to-nav` div contains links to other areas of the page. While some of these may be hidden, they still provide a useful guide for visitors who are not viewing your wiki through a conventional browser.

Using a conditional PHP statement, these links are only shown if needed. `<?php $this->msg('jumpto') ?>` retrieves the text as shown here:

```php
<?php if($this->data['showjumplinks']) { ?>
<div id="jump-to-nav">
<?php $this->msg('jumpto') ?>
<a href="#column-one">
<?php $this->msg('jumptonavigation') ?>
</a>,
<a href="#searchInput">
<?php $this->msg('jumptosearch') ?>
</a>
</div>
<?php } ?>
```

Page Anchors:
The links to your wiki's search box and navigation will work only if you have included the page anchors in the relevant place in your wiki's PHP template file.

Message Notification

When one of your wiki's users receive a new message on their talk page (for example, if you are logged in as "Richard", and a change is made to User_talk: Richard), a notification appears on the next page they view to tell them that a new message has been received. This notification appears in a div of class usermessage. The div contains a conditional statement in PHP, which only inserts the notification if a new message exists for the user:

```
<?php if($this->data['newtalk'] ) { ?>
<div class="usermessage">
<?php $this->html('newtalk')   ?>
</div>
<?php } ?>
```

So, if there is no new message for the user, no XHTML is generated. Otherwise, the following XHTML is generated by MediaWiki:

```
<div class="usermessage">
You have <a href=" index.php?title=User_talk:Admin&amp;redirect=no"
title="User talk:Admin">new messages</a> (<a href="index.
php?title=User_talk:Admin&amp;diff=cur" title="User talk:Admin">last
change</a>).
</div>
```

Pagetitle

The page title is inserted in the wiki page, if the page title is not empty. The following is MonoBook's lead in <h1> tags of class. .firstHeading:

```
<h1 class="firstHeading">
<?php $this->data['displaytitle']!=""?$this->html('title'):$this-
>text('title') ?>
</h1>
```

 Beware of over-inserting the page title as over-use could harm your wiki's search engine rankings.

Sitenotice

Because we need to check for the existence of a `sitenotice` before inserting it, we can use a conditional check, which inserts it if, and only if, the `sitenotice` is not empty. This is done in the same way as the 'new message' notification is inserted, above.

```
<?php if($this->data['sitenotice']) { ?>
<div id="siteNotice">
<?php $this->html('sitenotice') ?>
</div><?php } ?>
```

MediaWiki: Sitenotice

You can change your wiki's `sitenotice` content by editing the `MediaWiki:Sitenotice` page. You will need to be logged in as an administrator or sysop to edit this page.

Subtitle and Redirects

When a visitor goes to a page in your wiki that redirects to another page, a message is included beneath the page title to inform the visitor of the page from which he or she was redirected:

```
<div id="contentSub">
<?php $this->html('subtitle') ?>
</div>
```

The function highlighted above inserts this value in to the page in MediaWiki.

Tagline

The `tagline` function, highlighted below, inserts 'From JazzMeet' (or whatever your wiki's name is, as specified when you initialized your wiki) in to the wiki's page. In keeping with MonoBook's system of naming for the elements of wiki pages, the `tagline` is included within the #siteSub div:

```
<h3 id="siteSub">
<?php $this->msg('tagline') ?>
</h3>
```

Undelete

The `undelete` function inserts a link to restore an article you have deleted from the wiki as a user with the administrator privileges. This is inserted only if it is needed in the page:

```
<?php if($this->data['undelete']) { ?>
<div id="contentSub2">
<?php     $this->html('undelete') ?>
</div>
<?php } ?>
```

The default message text is "**View or restore one deleted edit**", as shown the following screenshot:

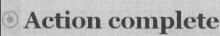

Footer

The footer links in your wiki are, as with the other menus and lists, inserted dynamically as an unordered list in XHTML, with an array (a list) of the links defined within the PHP file itself. The array specifies the links that should be included:

```
<ul id="f-list">
<?php
$footerlinks = array(
    'about', 'disclaimer',
);
foreach( $footerlinks as $aLink ) {
if( isset( $this->data[$aLink] ) && $this->data[$aLink] ) {
?>
<li id="<?php echo$aLink?>"><?php $this->html($aLink) ?></li>
<?php }
}
?>
</ul>
```

 Both isset($var) and $var will return false when var does not contain a value. So $this->data[$alink] is probably sufficient. We will leave isset there just in case, though.

The following code inserts the "about" and "disclaimer" links on the page:

```
<li id="about">
<a href="/richard.carter/book/v1/index.php/JazzMeet:About"
title="JazzMeet:About">About JazzMeet</a>
</li>
<li id="disclaimer">
<a href="/richard.carter/book/v1/index.php/JazzMeet:General_
disclaimer" title="JazzMeet:General disclaimer">Disclaimers</a>
</li>
```

Functions for the Interface

The interface area of MediaWiki is, as with the content area, generated through functions and variables that dynamically insert the logo, your wiki's navigation, and the footer links.

Logopath

The `<?php $this->text('logopath') ?>` function inserts the path of your wiki's logo, as defined by `$wgLogo` in `LocalSettings.php`. Depending on the value you have given this variable, it may be an absolute URL (for example, `http://www.example.com/images/logo.gif`), or a relative URL (for example, `images/logo.gif`).

Non- Special Pages

The first toolbox links to be inserted in the page are those for "normal" MediaWiki pages. So, we need a way of checking if the page is "special" (that is, prefixed with **Special**, for example, `Special:Recentchanges`):

```php
<?php if($this->data['notspecialpage']) { ?>
/*
code to be inserted if the page is not 'special' goes here
*/
} ?>
```

Whatlinkshere

The `whatlinkshere` feature provides a link to the page that lists pages every page on your wiki that links to the current page. This can also be inserted in to your MediaWiki template as follows:

```php
<li id="t-whatlinkshere"><a href="
<?php
echo htmlspecialchars($this->data['nav_urls']['whatlinkshere']['href'])?>"
<?php echo $skin->tooltipAndAccesskey('t-whatlinkshere') ?>
>
<?php $this->msg('whatlinkshere') ?>
</a>
</li>
```

Once the page is loaded, the XHTML in the page should look similar to the one given here:

```html
<li id="t-whatlinkshere">
<a href="index.php/Special:Whatlinkshere/JazzMeetDurham" title="List
of all wiki pages that link here [j]" accesskey="j">What links here</
a>
</li>
```

Recent Changes

We will add the link to the recent changes page link next, again within our conditional statement to check if the page is special:

```php
<?php if ( $this->data['nav_urls']['recentchangeslinked'] ) { ?>
<li id="t-recentchangeslinked">
<a href="
<?php echo htmlspecialchars($this->data['nav_urls']['recentchangeslink
ed']['href'])?>"
<?php echo $skin->tooltipAndAccesskey('t-recentchangeslinked') ?>
>
<?php $this->msg('recentchangeslinked') ?>
</a>
</li>
```

This PHP code results in XHTML for only one link:

```
<li id="t-recentchangeslinked">
<a href=" index.php/Special:Recentchangeslinked/JazzMeetDurham"
title="Recent changes in pages linked from this page [k]"
accesskey="k">Related changes</a>
</li>
```

Printable Version

The link to the printable version of the current page is a generated link. Obviously, this would need to be within the conditional statement to check that you are not generating a link to a printable version of a page that is a special page.

```php
if (!empty($this->data['nav_urls']['print']['href'])) { ?>
<li id="t-print">
<a href="<?php echo htmlspecialchars($this->data['nav_urls']['print']
['href'])?>"
<?php echo $skin->tooltipAndAccesskey('t-print') ?>>
<?php $this->msg('printableversion') ?>
</a></li>
<?php}
```

With a similar result to the previous examples, this code inserts a list item containing a link to the printable version of the page, assuming that the page is "non-special":

```
<li id="t-print">
<a href=" index.php?title=JazzMeetDurham&amp;printable=yes"
title="Printable version of this page [p]" accesskey="p">Printable
version</a>
</li>
```

Personal Tools

The personal tool links-those for your user page, talk page and your preferences-are also inserted on each page of your wiki as generated links, based on whether you are logged in to an account or not, and whether you have administrator privileges. The title is called in a similar manner to the one for the "views" section:

```
<h5>
<?php $this->msg('personaltools') ?>
</h5>
```

Again, the links for the personal tool-bar are inserted iteratively in an unordered list:

```
<ul>
<?php foreach($this->data['personal_urls'] as $key => $item) { ?>
<li id="pt-<?php echo Sanitizer::escapeId($key) ?>"<?php
if ($item['active']) { ?> class="active"<?php } ?>>
<a href="<?php echo htmlspecialchars($item['href']) ?>"
<?php echo $skin->tooltipAndAccesskey('pt-'.$key) ?>
<?php if(!empty($item['class'])) { ?>
class="<?php echo htmlspecialchars($item['class']) ?>"<?php } ?>>
<?php echo htmlspecialchars($item['text']) ?>
</a>
</li>
<?php} ?>
</ul>
```

Search

The title for the search feature in MediaWiki can be inserted in a header tag thus:

```
<h5>
<?php $this->msg('search') ?>
</h5>
```

The search form consists of one input field for the visitor's search term, and two inputs of type submit, one of which to search for the given phrase(s), we have hidden for JazzMeet using CSS. Of particular interest to us is <?php $this->text('searchaction') ?>, which inserts the needed action for the search form to function:

```
<form action="<?php $this->text('searchaction') ?>" id="searchform">
<input id="searchInput" name="search" type="text"<?php echo $skin->too
ltipAndAccesskey('search');
if( isset( $this->data['search'] ) ) {?> value="<?php $this-
>text('search') ?>"<?php } ?> />
```

```
<input type='submit' name="go" class="searchButton" id="searchGoButton
"value="<?php $this->msg('searcharticle') ?>" />
<input type='submit' name="fulltext" class="searchButton" id="mw-
searchButton" value="<?php $this->msg('searchbutton') ?>" />
</form>
```

This results in a change in the form `action` parameter, as follows:

```
<form action="index.php/Special:Search" id="searchform">
<!-- form contents -->
</form>
```

Views

The views section of MediaWiki lists the different views for the current page: the edit interface, the page's edit history, and any administrator actions available, such as delete and move.

Retrieving the title for this section (in <h5> tags, in both MonoBook and our JazzMeet template) requires a simple function call:

```
<h5>
<?php $this->msg('views') ?>
</h5>
```

To generate the list of relevant links for the page, the PHP gets a little more complex, with MediaWiki inserting them iteratively:

```
<ul>
<?php foreach($this->data['content_actions'] as $key => $tab) { ?>
<li id="ca-<?php echo Sanitizer::escapeId($key) ?>"
<?php if($tab['class']) { ?> class="<?php echo htmlspecialchars($tab['
class']) ?>"<?php } ?>>
<a href="<?php echo htmlspecialchars($tab['href']) ?>"<?php echo
$skin->tooltipAndAccesskey('ca-'.$key) ?>><?php
echo htmlspecialchars($tab['text']) ?>
</a>
</li>
<?php } ?>
</ul>
```

Logged in, and on a normal article page such as JazzMeetDurham, as used in the example below, this would generate content similar to the following, with each link's href, title, and accesskey parameters populated with the relevant information:

```
<h5>Views</h5>
<ul>
<li id="ca-nstab-main" class="selected">
<a href="index.php/JazzMeetDurham" title="View the content page [c]"
accesskey="c">Article</a>
</li>
<li id="ca-talk">
<a href="index.php/Talk:JazzMeetDurham" title="Discussion about the
content page [t]" accesskey="t">Discussion</a></li>
<li id="ca-edit">
<a href="index.php?title=JazzMeetDurham&amp;action=edit" title="You
can edit this page. Please use the preview button before saving. [e]"
accesskey="e">Edit</a>
</li>
<li id="ca-history">
<a href="index.php?title=JazzMeetDurham&amp;action=history"
 title="Past versions of this page. [h]" accesskey="h">History</a>
</li>
<li id="ca-watch">
<a href="index.php?title=JazzMeetDurham&amp;action=watch"  title="Add
this page to your watchlist [w]" accesskey="w">Watch</a></li>
</ul>
```

Toolbox

MediaWiki's toolbox contains links to a printable version of the current page, and links to other useful tools on your wiki:

```
<h5>
<?php $this->msg('toolbox') ?>
</h5>
```

This is where MediaWiki's template file gets very messy, as each link is inserted conditionally; that is, it is inserted if and only if it is required. This means, there are many "if" statements in this section.

Each list item inserted in a communal unordered list, which generates an XHTML similar to the following:

```
<ul>
<li id="t-whatlinkshere">
<a href=" Special:Whatlinkshere/Test" title="List of all wiki pages
```

```
that link here [j]" accesskey="j">What links here</a>
</li>
<li id="t-upload">
<a href="Special:Upload" title="Upload images or media files [u]"
accesskey="u">Upload file</a>
</li>
<li id="t-specialpages">
<a href="Special:Specialpages" title="List of all special pages [q]"
accesskey="q">Special pages</a>
</li>
</ul>
```

Loose Ends

There are a few commands that are useful if you are attempting to debug problems with your MediaWiki install, as well as a request to run any JavaScript associated with the page once the page has been loaded.

Bottomscripts

The "bottomscripts" command, `<?php $this->html('bottomscripts'); ?>`, inserts a call to run any JavaScript reliant on the loading of the page. This is best left towards the bottom of your template file, as including it higher up in your template file may make the JavaScript run before the page has been fully generated by MediaWiki.

Debugging

The debug function can be used to insert commented text in your template to help you debug MediaWiki:

```
<?php if ( $this->data['debug'] ): ?>
<!-- Debug output:
<?php $this->text( 'debug' ); ?>
-->
<?php endif; ?>
```

Debugging MediaWiki:

For more information on debugging MediaWiki, see `http://www.mediawiki.org/wiki/How_to_debug_MediaWiki`.

Reporttime

The "reporttime" function in MediaWiki, `<?php $this->html('reporttime') ?>`, inserts commented text in the page that reports the time taken to generate the page just before the `</body>` tag.

```
<!-- Served in 0.265 secs. -->
```

This is inserted in an HTML comment to prevent it being visible to your visitors, but still allows you to check whether there are any huge delays in the page loading.

Restoring Warnings

The `wfRestoreWarnings()` method call enables warnings to be displayed once the page has been generated. At the start of your skin file, if `wfSuppressWarnings()` is inserted before the HTML document type declaration, errors are disabled from being displayed in the page. This is a wise move with regards to the security, as it helps to prevent flaws that can be exploited to damage your wiki:

```
<?php
wfRestoreWarnings();}
}
?>
```

Advanced PHP Functions

By looking through the `SkinTemplate.php` file in your MediaWiki install's directory, you can find lots of useful functions to extend the information you can dynamically insert in your wiki pages.

Global Variables

The `SkinTemplate.php` file contains "global variables" that you can insert in your wiki page using this simple PHP:

```
<?php echo
$GLOBALS['name_of_global_variable'];
?>
```

The echo command inserts the value returned from the $GLOBALS that follows it. The following are the variables you can use:

- wgTitle inserts the current page's title.

- wgScript inserts your MediaWiki installation's script path. The script path is the part of the URL before your page title. For example, if your wiki was installed in the directory wiki/ on your website, the script path would be wiki/index.php.

- wgStylePath inserts your wiki's skins directory.

- wgContLanguageCode inserts the ISO language code of the content. In most cases, it will be "en" for English.

- wgMimeType inserts the MIME (Multipurpose Internet Mail Extensions) type of the content being returned. This is "text" or "html", by default.

- wgOutputEncoding inserts the character encoding type. The most frequent values for this are "UTF-8" and "ISO-8859-1".

- wgServer inserts the address of the server of your MediaWiki installation. For example, if your wiki is installed on www.example.com, wgServer returns http://www.example.com.

- wgArticlePath inserts the relative path of your wiki articles. For example, if your wiki is installed in the wiki directory, it would return wiki/index.php/$1. The $1 refers to the parameter of the article name.

Example: Dynamically Creating Linking Code

We will make use of some of the functions that were explained earlier to dynamically create the code that can be used by our wiki's visitors in order to link to the current page.

```
<label for="jazzmeet-link">Link to this page!</label>
<textarea name="jazzmeet-link" cols="35" rows="10">
<a href="
<?php echo $GLOBALS['wgServer']; ?><?php echo $GLOBALS['wgScript'];
?>/<?php echo $GLOBALS['wgTitle']; ?>
title="<?php echo $GLOBALS['wgTitle']; ?>">
<!--link text-->
'<?php echo $GLOBALS['wgTitle']; ?>' on JazzMeet
</a>
</textarea>
```

For the page `JazzMeetNewcastle` on our JazzMeet wiki, located at `www.jazzmeet.com/wiki/JazzMeetNewcastle`, this would generate something similar to the following screenshot:

```
Link to this page!
<a href="
http://www.jazzmeet.com/wiki/
index.php/Main Page"
title="Main Page">
<!--link text-->
'Main Page' on JazzMeet
</a>
```

Overview: Variables at a Glance

The `outputPage` function in the `includes/SkinTemplate.php` file gives us more options for content that we can insert in to our MediaWiki pages dynamically, some of which are included as an easy reference to the content covered in this chapter.

`$this->text($var)` will print the variable as plain text, whereas `$this->html($var)` will print the HTML content of the variable (where appropriate, and where possible). `$this->data($var)` is used to check whether or not the variable contains data.

"text" Variables

The "text" template variables can be accessed with the type "text" (see the following example). These include:

- `title`: This is the page's title.
- `pagetitle`: This is the page's title and your wiki's title (as set in `MediaWiki:Pagetitle`), concatenated.
- `pageclass`: This is the class assigned to the body of your wiki page. For the main page, this is `page-Main_Page`, although the syntax (that is, preceding page) can be removed quite easily by editing the `SkinTemplate.php` file.
- `articleid`: This is the numerical identifier of the article. The main Page's `articleid` is (usually) 1.
- `currevisionid`: This is the version number of the current version of the page.

- `skinname`: This is the name of the default skin for your wiki. This is '**JazzMeet**' for our case study.

- `stylename`: This is the directory of the current default skin. This is '**Jazzmeet**' for the JazzMeet wiki.

- `userpage`: This is the MediaWiki URL to the visitor's userpage. If you are logged in as "**Richard**", this is `User:Richard`. Also see "`userpageurl`".

- `viewcount`: This is a message that tells you how many times the current page has been accessed. The message reads, "**This page has been accessed 'x' times.**"

These variables can be inserted into the page in a way similar to the global variables described earlier. To insert the page title in the page without using the global variable, you can use the following:

```
<?php $this->text('title') ?>
```

"html" Variables

The "`html`" variables can be used in a way similar to the "`text`" variables that were described earlier (and, indeed, can be requested as "`text`" variables, with varying results). These include the following:

- `catlinks`: This links to the page's relevant categories (if any).

- `headlinks`: These are the meta keywords and favicon link in the header.

- `userpageurl`: This is the relative URL to the vistors's userpage. It returns something similar to: `wiki/index.php/User:Richard`.

Calling the "`html`" function before retrieving the values ensures that the returned value is displayed as HTML. If we want to insert another instance of the page's category links into the page, we can use the following:

```
<?php $this->html('catlinks') ?>
```

This inserts the relevant HTML for the page's categories in the following format, assuming the page's only category is called "Test":

```
<p class='catlinks'>
<a href="wiki/index.php/Special:Categories" title="Special:
Categories">Category</a>: <span dir='ltr'><a href="wiki/index.
php?title=Category:Test&amp;action=edit" title="Category:Test">Test</
a></span>
</p>
```

Summary

In this chapter we discussed the various functions for inserting useful information in your wiki dynamically. This included the following:

- Functions for retrieving and inserting data from both variables and functions
- Inserting global variables in your MediaWiki template

In the next chapter, we will discuss adding decorative elements to your wiki, and integrating social bookmarking websites in your wiki.

Adding Decorative Elements

6

The design of our JazzMeet wiki is preliminarily complete, but we can enhance it in terms of user-friendliness, by adding decorative elements. In this chapter, we will cover the following:

- The decorative elements you can use in your wiki
- The techniques you can use in your wiki to draw your visitor's focus both toward elements and away from elements

Decorative Elements

A decorative element is not essential to your wiki's skin, but adds some value to it. This value could give your wiki a certain attitude or a distinctive element over a competitor's wiki, or help your visitors perform some task on your wiki, such as finding the information they are looking for using the search box feature.

When to Use Decorative Elements

It is important to use the decorative elements in your MediaWiki skin sparingly, so as not to detract from the wiki's content, which is why most of your visitors are on your wiki in the first place.

Having said that, a white page with black text is not very welcoming for your visitors, and decorative elements can help make your wiki more visitor-friendly.

As a general guide, it is probably OK to use decorative elements when:

- Your page is a somewhat sparse
- Something on your page needs more focus than it currently has
- The wrong elements on your page have too much focus (for example, through poor choice in layout), and you need to draw attention to other elements on the page

Whilst it is always a good idea to plan what goes where before you design your MediaWiki skin, this is not always practical. For example, you may find that once your wiki has been up and running for a while, you want to add or change the decorative elements based on comments from your visitors, or want to make changes based on analysis of your website's statistics.

Focus-Drawing Techniques

You can draw focus to an element on your wiki by using one or more of the following techniques:

- Suggestion of movement, including the use of arrows
- Color contrast
- Diagonal lines
- Indentation
- Padding
- Size
- Ordering
- Depth, and the impression of 3D

Suggestion of Movement

Our eyes are designed to respond to movement. Anything that appears to be moving (or actually is moving), will tend to draw your visitors' focus.

Movement and Advertisements:

Beware of making things that look like animated banner adverts, as your visitors may associate these with advertisements and ignore them. Refer to: http://www.useit.com/alertbox/9709a.html.

For example, by applying a motion blur to each of the sponsors' logos, we can attract our visitors' attention to them:

On the other hand, this motion blur makes the logos less legible for our visitors. So we should clearly exercise caution here.

Drawing Focus with Arrows

A good way to suggest movement is with the use of arrows. The tip of the arrow will drive your visitors' attention towards whatever it is pointing at, as we can see in the following example:

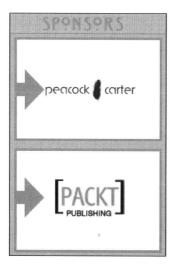

The arrows can help to guide visitors through your wiki, and help to enforce the hierarchy of the content. For example, let's assume that our first sponsor was paying more than the second, and we wanted our visitors to view these. We could use arrows to suggest to our visitors the order in which they view our sponsors' logos, and thus, theoretically at least, the first sponsor gains the most attention from our visitors:

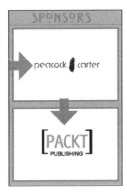

Alternatively, we can reverse the arrows to suggest a reversal in the hierarchy of the sponsors' logos, such that the lower logo is given a greater focus than the first:

Color Contrast

The use of color and contrast in your design can also help to tell your visitors what is more important on your wiki.

If your design is predominantly blue, an orange element will stand out more than a different shade of orange, as orange and blue are on opposite sides of the "color wheel".

 For this technique to work well, you need to have the majority of your design in a single color, or a variation of that color.

The Color Wheel

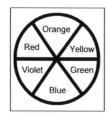

Let's assume that the JazzMeet's sponsors (in the right-hand column of our original design) weren't happy with the percentage of visitors who visited their websites from our wiki. The beige border surrounding the logos (#BEB798) was originally designed to indicate to JazzMeet's visitors that the sponsors' logos on the wiki were not very important to the page content.

We can change the contrast of the sponsors' logos by changing the border color that surrounds them from beige (close to orange on the color wheel) to its opposite on the color wheel, a shade of blue.

Grayscale and Monotone

Using grayscale and monotone images can be just as striking as the use
of vivid colors. This is illustrated by Khoi Vinh on his personal blog, Subtraction
(`http://www.subtraction.com`):

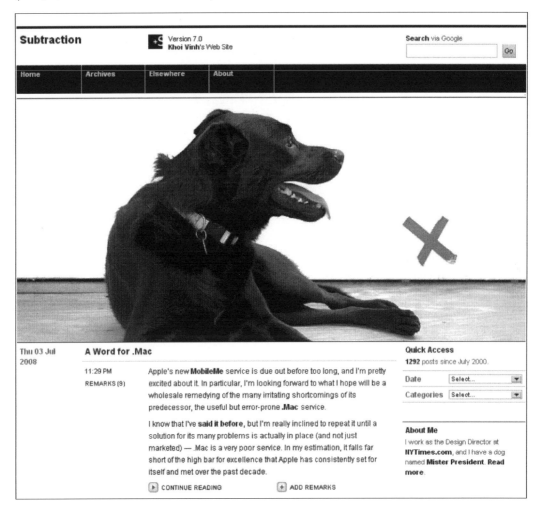

This effect is demonstrated on JazzMeet's sponsor logos in the following screenshot. As JazzMeet's design is quite colorful, the effect is significantly reduced:

Diagonal Lines

Diagonal lines, or an image with a diagonal edge, will draw more focus from your visitors than the same content with straight lines. Let us say that we do not like the blue borders on JazzMeet's sponsor logos, as they don't really fit our color scheme well.

We can attract our visitors' attention towards the sponsor logos, by altering the borders to contain diagonal elements:

Size

This is possibly the most obvious way to draw attention to something in your wiki's design—by making it larger. One of the reasons why the newspaper headings grab your attention is that they are larger than the surrounding content.

Thus, making the sponsors' logos smaller, in this case half of the original size, reduces their ability to be noticed by visitors to the JazzMeet wiki.

Indentation

You can establish a visual hierarchy between your wiki's blocks of content through the use of indentation and padding. Generally, indentation is used to reduce the importance of an element within a page. For example, in the table of contents, the more indented a section's heading is, the less important it is.

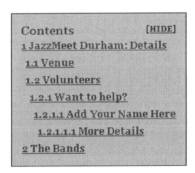

In the table of contents just shown, indentation helps to make it clear that section 1.1 ('Venue') is more important than section 1.2.1.1.1 ("More Details").

Padding

Padding is the space between elements. We can also make use of the `margin` attribute in CSS to achieve the same effect.

Padding and margin both refer to the space around an object. The difference is that padding is a part of the object whereas margin is not.

For example, if we still wanted to draw attention to JazzMeet's sponsors, we could have more space ("padding") between the two sponsor logos:

The whitespace is striking. So many posters and print advertising campaigns, especially for things such as perfumes and clothing, will contain only minimal content and a lot of empty space, because it attracts attention.

However, in a web design, as opposed to a print design, too much whitespace could annoy your visitors by spreading the information they need over a larger portion of "screen real estate". This means that your visitors could have to do a lot of unnecessary scrolling.

Do not over-do it:

The trick with any of the above techniques is to use them sparingly. The overuse of any one of them, or a combination of them, will result in your visitors not knowing where to focus their attention.

Order

The order of elements on a web page or any document will also have an affect on the amount of attention your visitors pay to them. In most Western countries, where we read from left to right, something at the top-left of a web page is much more likely to attract our attention than something at the bottom-right.

Thus, website footers contain information that most of the visitors wouldn't be very interested in, such as copyright details, and information on what powers the website (in our case, MediaWiki).

In the same way, let us say that one of our sponsors suddenly donates a lot of money towards JazzMeet's hosting costs, and we want to reward them by giving them more precedence in the sponsor section of our wiki.

We can re-order the sponsors' logos, so the sponsor who donated the most money or resources to JazzMeet appears at the top of the sponsors list.

Depth and the Third Dimension

Much like movement, our brains are designed to perceive depth; that is, we seem programmed with an innate ability to see in three dimensions.

This is especially effective on the Internet and in print, as a web page (or a magazine page) is two-dimensional. Adding a perceived third dimension to a web page can greatly enhance its power to catch your visitors' attention.

A good example of the human brain being able to perceive 3D is Ames' Window, available through Professor Richard Gregory's website, at: `http://www.richardgregory.org/experiments/video/ames_window.htm`.

A more recent and web-related depth example is the website for Silverback (`http://www.silverbackapp.com`):

Interestingly, the vines are layered (using the `z-index` property in CSS and transparent PNGs) to give the viewer a notion of depth. The closer the vines are meant to be, the more blurred they are.

 Whilst the concept of creating depth with multiple overlaying divs is interesting, the same effect could quite easily be achieved by using a single, repeating background image.

In a similar way, we can attract JazzMeet visitors' focus to the sponsors' logos by creating a sense of depth by using a 3D affect on each of the logo "boxes".

Focus-Lessening Techniques

Lowering the visual impact of some of your wiki's elements to give more precedence to the others can be done in two ways.

Firstly, you can simply adjust the visual impact of the elements in your design using the focus-drawing techniques that we discussed. This will place the more important elements at a higher level of your wiki design's visual hierarchy.

 For major changes in the focus of elements on your wiki, this probably isn't suitable. As a result, you may want to reconsider your wiki's overall layout and design.

Secondly, you can use some other ideas for getting the attention of your wiki's visitors. These are as follows:

- lower contrast, both within the element, and in relation to the other elements
- smaller sizes, without making the element's content unreadable; it may be possible to reduce its size, and, thus, the impact
- less indentation and padding

Summary

In this chapter we covered various decorative elements in websites, and their application to your MediaWiki wiki. This included drawing the focus of the visitors through the use of the following:

- Size
- Contrast
- Diagonal planes of vision
- Indentation
- Movement
- Depth

We also learnt that it is important to assign importance to our content and other elements, as it adds to the hierarchy of your website's content.

Dynamic CSS and JavaScript

7

Many websites make use of JavaScript to help their visitors. JavaScript is a client-side scripting language, which means that it runs on your visitors' computers, and not your server. In other words, the elements of your wiki can be manipulated without the wiki page being reloaded.

Less is more with JavaScript

JavaScript is an excellent tool, but be careful to use it to enhance your website. Also be sure that your wiki's primary functionality, which includes being able to add, edit, and manipulate pages, is still easily done for those visitors who do not have JavaScript enabled or installed.

In this chapter, we will cover integrating some JavaScript into the JazzMeet. This includes the following:

- Manipulating the edit page so that you can edit your wiki's content in a "light box"
- Manipulating tables in your wiki through "Tablecloth"

Inline Edit Interface

Some of JazzMeet's regular contributors may find it easier to have the edit interface appear inline. We can achieve this by using JavaScript.

We have quite a few choices when it comes to providing a suitable solution for this functionality. We will assess ThickBox, Lightbox 2, and GreyBox, all of which have slightly different features and implementations.

ThickBox

ThickBox (`http://jquery.com/demo/thickbox/`) is a JavaScript "widget" that makes use of the jQuery library:

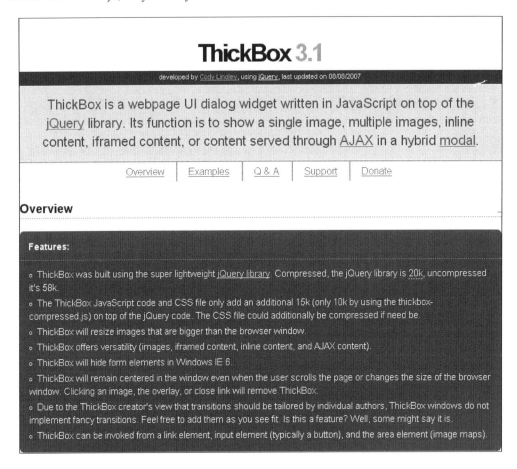

What does ThickBox Support?

We can use ThickBox with images, content within iframes, and AJAX-based content. ThickBox also supports inline content (that is, content within the page that you are linking, as seen in the following screenshot), although this is not of interest to us in this application. Unlike Lightbox, ThickBox can also be used with Flash videos and games.

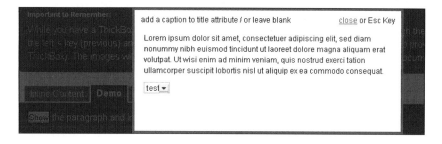

ThickBox's Features

ThickBox allows for its invocation from three elements: links, inputs (for example, submit buttons), and image maps. It will also automatically resize images that are too big to fit comfortably within the viewer's browser window.

To invoke Thickbox, the triggering item, for example a link to another page, needs to have been assigned a class of .thickbox.

 The triggering class can be configured in the ThickBox JavaScript files. For more details, refer to the ThickBox documentation.

As with GreyBox and Lightbox, ThickBox allows the "window" to be closed when the user clicks the "close" button, or when the Escape key is pressed.

GreyBox

GreyBox (http://www.orangoo.com/labs/GreyBox/) has similar functionality to ThickBox.

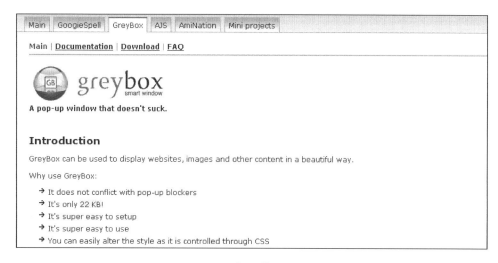

What does GreyBox Support?

GreyBox can be used to display single images, webpages, and webpage galleries.

GreyBox's Features

GreyBox is invoked by adding a `rel` attribute to the link to be used in conjunction with it. GreyBox is more complex to use than Lightbox or Thickbox as the type of pop-up that needs to be displayed has to be defined within the `rel` attribute, as per the documentation on the GreyBox website.

This, however, allows for greater flexibility, with galleries of images gaining a navigation bar at the top of the screen:

Websites linked to GreyBox are displayed a bit differently by default, in a browser-like window. For instance, look at the Google UK homepage in the following screenshot:

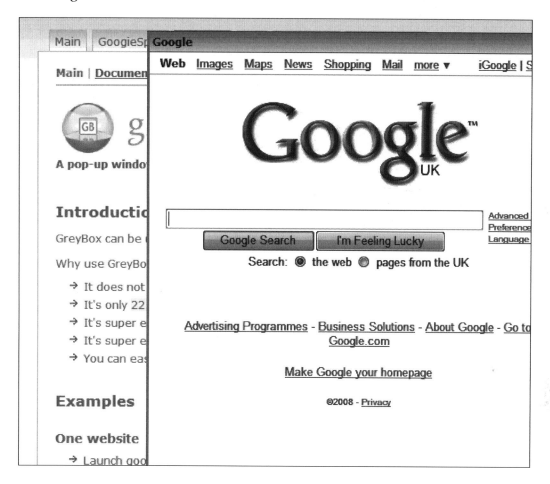

Lightbox 2

Lightbox 2 (`http://www.lokeshdhakar.com/projects/lightbox2/`) is the work of Lokesh Dhakar, and similar provides functionality to GreyBox and ThickBox, as its focus is on being easy to install and use.

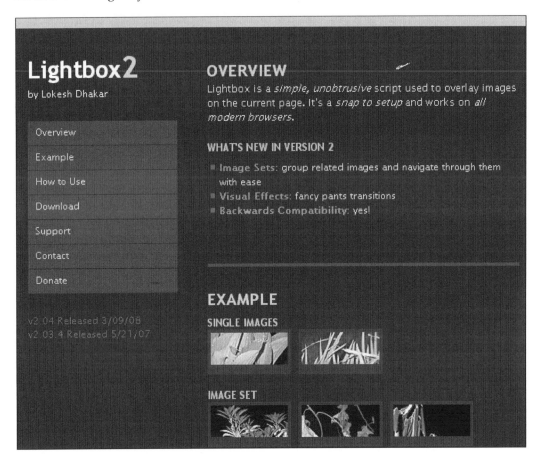

What does Lightbox Support?

Lightbox has built-in transitions between images, although it does not support iframes (well, at least not yet), or Flash files, which GreyBox does.

Lightbox's Features

Lightbox has the ability to display both images and web pages:

Lightbox also supports images in galleries:

Invocation of Lightbox, once it is installed, is achieved by adding a `rel` attribute to the linked item, but in a much simpler fashion than GreyBox.

Lightbox 2 Wins

There are some CSS-based options for adding the ability to have content in your wiki pop-up over the current page. However, these have patchy support across browsers, and involve adding additional HTML to the page, unnecessarily bloating it.

On the basis of this, and given that Lightbox is used by an existing MediaWiki extension, we will be using Lightbox 2 to pop up the edit interface for our visitors to use.

Installing Lightbox 2

There are a few steps that need to be followed to install and configure Lightbox 2 (version 2.04). They are as follows:

- Downloading and publishing the relevant JavaScript files to your own server
- Linking to these files in your wiki's head section
- Appending the Lightbox CSS to your current MediaWiki skin CSS
- Making changes to your wiki's HTML to tell Lightbox where it is used

Script Files for Header

There are currently three script files that need to be included in your wiki's `<head>` section, using the HTML below:

```
<script type="text/javascript" src="js/prototype.js"></script>
<script type="text/javascript" src="js/scriptaculous.js?load=effects,b
uilder"></script>
<script type="text/javascript" src="js/lightbox.js"></script>
```

You will then need to find these files on the Lightbox 2 website (`http://www.lokeshdhakar.com/projects/lightbox2/`), and upload them to your wiki's hosting account.

Be sure to change the paths of the JavaScript files (highlighted above) to their location on your server.

Lightbox CSS

You will require CSS to style the way the pop-up appears. This stylesheet is available on the Lightbox 2 website. You can do one of the three things with the Lightbox CSS:

- Append it to your wiki's existing skin CSS file
- Import it from your existing wiki's CSS file
- Link to it as a separate file in your wiki's head section

If you append it to your wiki's existing CSS file, it can bloat your existing style, and make it harder to read. On the other hand, importing the stylesheet from your existing stylesheet or linking to it as a separate stylesheet (using the `<style type="text/css"><!--@import stylesheet.css--></style>`) means that the browser has to make another HTTP request to the server. This could increase the loading time for your wiki.

The latter two options—of importing the style in another stylesheet, and importing it separately within your wiki's header—are among the better options if you want to make use of Lightbox (or any of its equivalents) in the other MediaWiki skins available to your wiki's visitors (such as MonoBook).

Let's assume that we will not have to work with the CSS for JazzMeet in any significant way. Once we have finished the JazzMeet skin, we will opt for appending the Lightbox style to our existing style for JazzMeet.

rel="lightbox"

The final step in using Lightbox is to add the attribute `rel='lightbox'` to the link tag:

```
<a href='http://www.example.com'>Example.com</a>
```

After adding the relevant `rel` attribute, we have the following:

```
<a rel='lightbox' href='http://www.example.com'>Example.com</a>
```

Because MediaWiki dynamically inserts the page view options such as "edit", "history", and "talk" into the page from an array, we need to insert a bit of PHP into the `JazzMeet.php` skin template file, to check if the link being inserted is the "edit page" link.

Identifying the "edit" link

Firstly, we identify the section of the MediaWiki template that inserts the "Views" option links in the page. This starts with `<?php foreach($this->data['content_actions'] as $key => $tab) { ?>`.

The code that needs to be inserted is highlighted below, and consists of an "if" statement to check the "key" value of the array. If this is "edit" (that is, this is the "edit page" link), then we insert the code `rel='lightbox'` in the link tag.

```
<li id="ca-<?php echo Sanitizer::escapeId($key) ?>" <?php
if($tab['class'])
    {
?> class="<?php echo htmlspecialchars($tab['class']) ?>" <?php
}
?>
><a href="<?php echo htmlspecialchars($tab['href']) ?>"
```

```php
<?php
   if( $key == 'edit' )
{
?> rel="lightbox" <?php
}?>
<?php echo $skin->tooltipAndAccesskey('ca-'.$key) ?>><?php
echo htmlspecialchars($tab['text']) ?></a></li>
<?php} ?>
```

You should now be able to edit a page in the JazzMeet wiki in a Lightbox window. Because the edit page is quite a large file, it will probably take more time to load. This, in turn should cause the display of a "loading" animation while you are waiting.

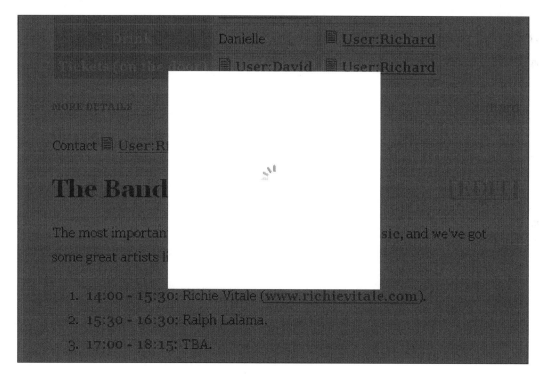

Once the page has been loaded, the white content container should expand to a width suitable for the edit interface. As the full edit page is loaded, the navigation and header areas are also loaded and displayed (but not shown in the screenshot below):

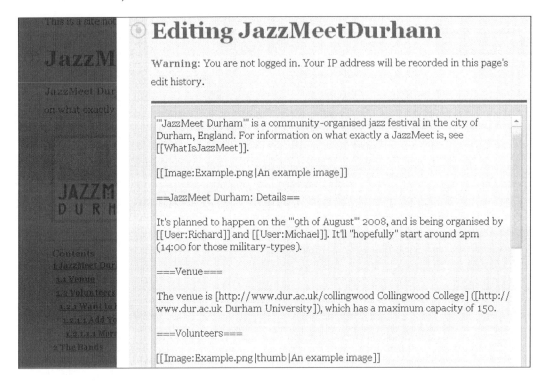

Customizing Lightbox 2

There are quite a few aspects of Lightbox that can be changed, including the following:

- The images, such as the loading graphic and the close button
- The CSS relevant to the Lightbox
- The level of transparency
- The caption text

Changing Lightbox Graphics

To give the loading graphic a more JazzMeet-themed look, we can use an animation of musical notes:

For example, instead of just the words "loading, please wait" your visitors will be expecting some sort of animation to inform them that the requested content is still being loaded. You can use non-animated graphics as the loading graphic too.

The other images you can alter are the "next" and "previous" button graphics, and the "close" button. These are easily found in the Lightbox 2 download package.

Changing Lightbox CSS

The CSS for Lightbox is quite compact. A few CSS ids and classes are defined within it, including the following:

- `#overlay` fills the screen with a semi-transparent effect when the Lightbox is activated.

- `#lightbox` is the container for the image or file in Lightbox.

- `#lightboxImage` is the image or file in Lightbox itself.

- `#imageDataContainer` contains the "next", "previous" and "close" buttons. It also contains the image or file caption.

For better compatibility of Lightbox with JazzMeet, we can change the background color of the overlay to dark brown (rather than the default black):

```
#overlay{
position: absolute;
top: 0;
left: 0;
z-index: 90;
width: 100%;
height: 500px;
background-color: #38230C;
}
```

Changing Lightbox Captions

With Lightbox 2, you can group the Lightbox contents together in the following manner:

```
<a href='image1.gif' rel='lightbox[group1]'>Item 1</a>
<a href='image2.gif' rel='lightbox[group1]'>Item 2</a>
```

When a gallery of images is displayed using Lightbox in the way just mentioned, Lightbox will insert a caption, for example, "Image 2 of 4", beneath the image. You can alter the text of this caption by altering the labelImage and labelOf variables in the lightbox.js file. The default settings are shown here:

```
labelImage: "Image",
labelOf: "of"
```

If we want to internationalize JazzMeet, we need to translate this to Italian. For example, "Image 1 of 3" would read "l'immagine 1 di 3".

```
labelImage: "l'immagine",
labelOf: "di"
```

LightboxThumbs

We can also use a functionality provided by LightBox to allow thumbnail images within our wiki to be opened within the page.

Lightbox 2 comes to our rescue here yet again, alongside the LightboxThumbs MediaWiki extension (`http://www.mediawiki.org/wiki/Extension:LightboxThumbs`).

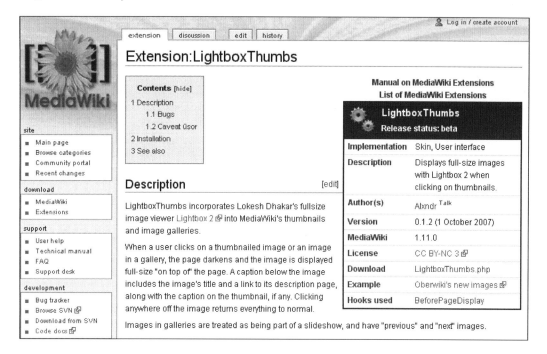

Installing LightboxThumbs

Installing LightboxThumbs is quite simple. You need to follow these steps:

- Save the `LightboxThumbs.php` file in the `extensions` directory of your MediaWiki installation. The file is provided on the Extensions page on `MediaWiki.org`.

- Inform MediaWiki that you are expecting the LightboxThumbs extension to be present by adding the code `requires_once("$IP/extensions/LightboxThumbs.php")` to your `LocalSettings.php` file.

- Install Lightbox.

The Result

We should now be able to see a larger version of images and photographs uploaded on our wiki when we click on the thumbnail version of images embedded within our wiki's content:

Tables: Making Data easier to read

As JazzMeet will be organising jazz gigs and events around the world in MediaWiki's collaborative environment, we will have a lot of HTML tables of data. These may include details such as who is organizing what and who is attending. In large tables, it can be easy to lose focus of the row or column that you were looking at, but we can use JavaScript scripts such as Tablecloth to enhance the visitors' experiences.

Tablecloth (`http://cssglobe.com/lab/tablecloth/`) is a JavaScript-based feature that highlight the row and column of a table that you are currently hovering over.

The script also assigns a class of `.odd` to the odd rows in the table, and `.even` to the even rows in the table.

Installing Tablecloth

The Tablecloth script needs to be installed in a way similar to Lightbox 2, that is, by linking to the JavaScript files in your wiki template's `<head>` section, and by adding the Tablecloth CSS to your existing CSS.

To link to the JavaScript files, you will need to add the following lines in the `<head>` section of your wiki (assuming that the Tablecloth JavaScript file is in the `skins/tc/` directory):

```
<script type="text/javascript" src="skins/tc/tablecloth.js"></script>
```

You will also need to include the Tablecloth CSS, either by linking to it in the head of the document, or by appending it to the existing CSS for your MediaWiki template. For the same reasons discussed earlier, we will simply append the Tablecloth CSS to our existing JazzMeet CSS file, in `skins/jazzmeet/main.css`.

Customizing Tablecloth

We can customize Tablecloth's CSS in order to match JazzMeet's color scheme (red, beige, and brown). Tablecloth defines a number of styles that allow you to customize the way tables are displayed on your website. These include the following:

- `.selected` is applied to the table cell that is currently selected (try clicking a table cell).
- `.empty` affects empty table cells.
- `.over` is used to identify the cells that are currently being hovered over.
- `.odd` and `.even` are used to distinguish between the odd and even rows in the table.

 Tablecloth was designed to work on websites that use HTML tables for tabular data only. However, by default, MediaWiki's table of contents (`#toc`) uses a table, so Tablecloth will affect its styling too.

We need to remove the styling that is provided by Tablecloth, as the JazzMeet skin already defines it. In particular, we need to remove the "`width: 100%`" that Tablecloth applies to the table element, as this will cause the table of contents to stretch to the full width of the content area of the JazzMeet design.

The Result: Highlighted Tables

The tables will now reflect our color scheme, and will be highlighted when the visitors with JavaScript enabled hover over the cells. As you can see, only the horizontal cells, and not the vertical cells, are highlighted.

In the example below, the table cell with "Danielle" is highlighted as its content is the one being hovered over, and the "Drink" and "User:Richard" cells are also highlighted, but less so than the cell being hovered over. Refer to the following screenshot:

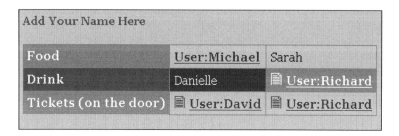

Summary

In this chapter, we covered the following:

- Various implementations of the popular JavaScript pop-ups such as ThickBox and GreyBox
- Using Lightbox to help your wiki flow better for your visitors
- Using Tablecloth for tabular data, to help highlight your visitors' focus in large amounts of data

We also covered topics that ensure we're not needlessly adding features that rely on JavaScript to the detriment of our wiki's visitors who do not have JavaScript enabled or installed.

With JavaScript libraries such as jQuery and `script.aculo.us`, adding new features and enhancing your wiki is quite easy.

8
Social Networking and MediaWiki

The MediaWiki skin for JazzMeet seems good, but we can still add certain things to our wiki to make it stand out. In this chapter, we will discuss the following:

- Integrating Twitter feeds in to your wiki's template
- Embedding and styling YouTube videos in your wiki
- Using social bookmarking services such as Furl and Facebook

Integrating Twitter with MediaWiki

Twitter (`http://www.twitter.com`) is a micro-blogging service that allows users to convey the world (or at least the small portion of it on Twitter) what they are doing, in messages of 140 characters or less.

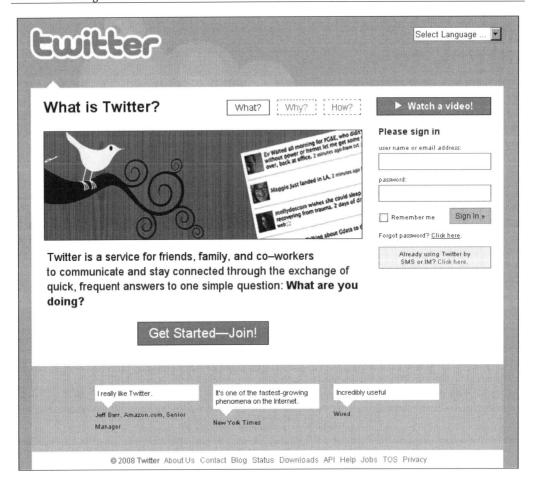

It is possible to embed these messages in external websites, which is what we will be doing for JazzMeet. We can use the updates to inform our wiki's visitors of the latest JazzMeet being held across the world, and they can send a response to the JazzMeet Twitter account.

Shorter Links

Because Twitter only allows posts of up to 140 characters, many Twitter users make use of URL-shortening services such as Tiny URL (`http://tinyurl.com`), and notlong (`http://notlong.com`) to turn long web addresses into short, more manageable URLs. Tiny URL assigns a random URL such as `http://tinyurl.com/3ut9p4`, while notlong allows you to pick a free sub-domain to redirect to your chosen address, such as `http://asgkasdgadg.notlong.com`.

Twitter automatically shortens web addresses in your posts.

Creating a Twitter Account

Creating a Twitter account is quite easy. Just fill in the username, password, and email address fields, and submit the registration form, once you have read and accepted the terms and conditions. If your chosen username is free, your account is created instantly.

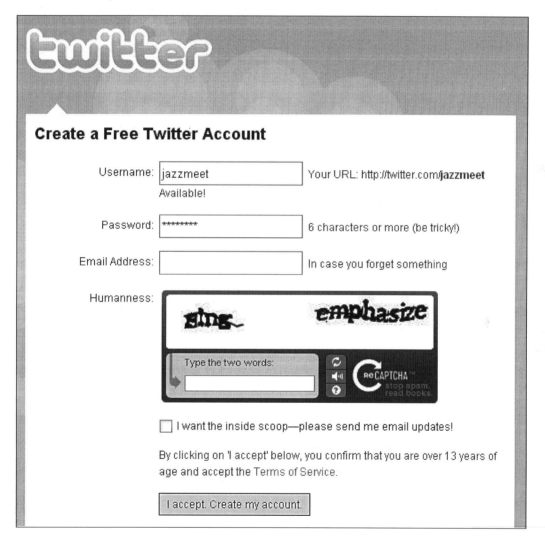

Once your account has been created, you can change the settings such as your display name and your profile's background image, to help blur the distinction between your website and your Twitter profile. Colors can be specified as "hex" values under the **Design** tab of your Twitter account's settings section. The following color codes change the link colors to our JazzMeet's palette of browns and reds:

JazzMeet (MediaWiki)

| Account | Password | Devices | Notices | Picture | Design |

Design Your Twitter

Below are the current design settings for your Twitter account. You can change, preview, save, or restore to factory default settings any time.

○ Use the Twitter default style
◉ Use my custom style below

Background Color: `BEB798`

Background Image: ☐ Use background image (Twitter Clouds)   ☐ Tile

[   ] [Choose...]

Images must be smaller than 800k. GIF, JPG, PNG.

Text Color: `000000`

Name Color: `8C1425`

Link Color: `8C1425`

Sidebar Fill Color: `E6E4D8`

Sidebar Border Color: `8C1425`

[Save]

As you can see in the screenshot, JazzMeet's Twitter profile now looks a little more like the JazzMeet wiki. By doing this, the visitors catching up with JazzMeet's events on Twitter will not be confused by a sudden change in color scheme:

Embedding Twitter Feeds in MediaWiki

Twitter provides a few ways to embed your latest posts in to your own website(s); simply log in and go to `http://www.twitter.com/badges`.

- Flash: With this option you can show just your posts, or your posts and your friends' most recent posts on Twitter.

- HTML and JavaScript: You can configure the code to show between 1 and 20 of your most recent Twitter posts.

As JazzMeet isn't really the sort of wiki the visitors would expect to find on Flash, we will be using the HTML and JavaScript version. You are provided with the necessary code to embed in your website or wiki. We will add it to the JazzMeet skin template, as we want it to be displayed on every page of our wiki, just beneath our sponsor links. Refer to the following code:

```
<div id="twitter_div">
<h2 class="twitter-title">Twitter Updates</h2>
<ul id="twitter_update_list">
</ul>
</div>
<script type="text/javascript" src="http://twitter.com/javascripts/
blogger.js"></script>
<script type="text/javascript" src="http://twitter.com/statuses/user_
timeline/jazzmeet.json?callback=twitterCallback2&count=5"></script>
```

The JavaScript given at the bottom of the code can be moved just above the </body> tag of your wiki's skin template. This will help your wiki to load other important elements of your wiki before the Twitter status.

 You will need to replace "jazzmeet" in the code with your own Twitter username, otherwise you will receive JazzMeet's Twitter updates, and not your own.

It is important to leave the unordered list of ID `twitter_update_list` as it is, as this is the element the JavaScript code looks for to insert a list item containing each of your twitter messages in the page.

Styling Twitter's HTML

We need to style the Twitter HTML by adding some CSS to change the colors and style of the Twitter status code:

```
#twitter_div {
background: #FFF;
border: 3px #BEB798 solid;
color: #BEB798;
margin: 0;
padding: 5px;
width: 165px;
}
#twitter_div a {
color: #8D1425 !important;
}
ul#twitter_update_list {
list-style-type: none;
margin: 0;
padding: 0;
}
#twitter_update_list li {
color: #38230C;
display: block;
}
h2.twitter-title {
color: #BEB798;
font-size: 100%;
}
```

There are only a few CSS IDs and classes that need to be taken care of. They are as follows:

- `#twitter_div` is the element that contains the Twitter feeds.

- `#twitter_update_list` is the ID applied to the unordered list. Styling this affects how your Twitter feeds are displayed.

- `.twitter-title` is the class applied to the Twitter feed's `<h2>` heading (which you can remove, if necessary).

Our wiki's skin for JazzMeet now has JazzMeet's Twitter feed embedded in the right-hand column, allowing visitors to keep up-to-date with the latest JazzMeet news.

Inserting Twitter as Page Content

MediaWiki does not allow JavaScript to be embedded in a page via the "edit" function, so you won't be able to insert a Twitter status feed directly in a page unless it is in the template itself. Even if you inserted the relevant JavaScript links into your MediaWiki skin template, they are relevant only for one Twitter profile ("jazzmeet", in our case).

YouTube in MediaWiki

YouTube (http://youtube.com) is a video sharing website that allows registered users to upload videos, and allows visitors to watch streamed videos that are categorized by tags. A feature useful to JazzMeet is that the videos can be embedded in external websites, by inserting the code provided on the video's page in to your own website. The code looks similar to the following example:

```
<object width="425" height="355"><param name="movie" value="http://
www.youtube.com/v/U4FAKRpUCYY&hl=en"></param><param name="wmode"
value="transparent"></param><embed src="http://www.youtube.
com/v/U4FAKRpUCYY&hl=en" type="application/x-shockwave-flash"
wmode="transparent" width="425" height="355"></embed></object>
```

This isn't particularly useful for MediaWiki, though, since you don't (generally) want videos in the template itself, but in the content area, where the HTML is presented as text within the document:

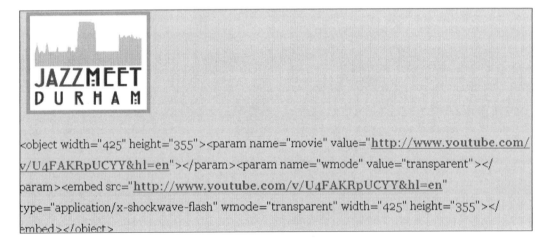

MediaWiki Extension: VideoFlash

We can overcome this problem with the use of an extension for MediaWiki called VideoFlash (http://www.mediawiki.org/wiki/Extension:VideoFlash). VideoFlash allows videos from a number of popular video websites, including YouTube and Google Video, to be embedded in your MediaWiki wiki with relative ease.

Installing VideoFlash

The instructions for installing VideoFlash are included on the website, but we will go through installing them on our JazzMeet wiki for clarity. Firstly, you will need to create a file called `videoflash.php` in the `extensions` directory of your MediaWiki installation. You should copy and paste the code provided in the extension's page on MediaWiki's website into this file.

Secondly, you will need to add a line of code at the end of your `LocalSettings.php` file, which is usually located in your MediaWiki's installation's root directory. If MediaWiki is installed at `http://www.example.com/wiki/`, you should be able to find `LocalSettings.php` at `http://www.example.com/wiki/LocalSettings.php`. The earlier versions of MediaWiki close the file with `?>`: the `require_once` statement below needs to be above this "end of file" marker:

```
require_once("extensions/videoflash.php");
```

This tells MediaWiki that you have installed the VideoFlash extension, and helps you to find the relevant file.

Embedding YouTube Videos in Page Content

If any visitor wants to embed the video located at `http://www.youtube.com/watch?v=U4FAKRpUCYY`, they can now do so by inserting the following wiki-markup in a MediaWiki page on the JazzMeet wiki:

```
<videoflash>U4FAKRpUCYY</videoflash>
```

The page should now display the relevant YouTube video.

Embedding Videos from other Video Providers

Google videos can be embedded with a similar code once the VideoFlash MediaWiki extension has been installed:

```
<videoflash type="googlevideo">U4FAKRpUCYY</videoflash>
```

Telling your Visitors

It is true that videos can be embedded into your wiki, but your visitors need to know that they can be embedded. There are two ways of conveying this information to your visitors. Either display the `Help:Editing` page, which is linked to the edit interface, or edit the text of the edit interface to inform your wiki's visitors that the ability to add videos from services such as YouTube is available.

The edit interface's text is similar to the one shown here:

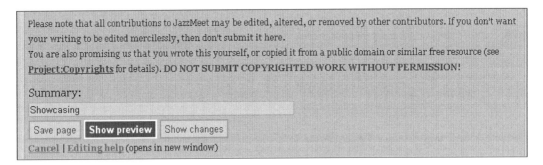

To alter the text in the edit interface, go to `MediaWiki:Copyrightwarning` or `MediaWiki:Copyrightwarning2`. This text is displayed directly above the edit summary box and the submission button for the edit. We will add the following HTML to `MediaWiki:Copyrightwarning2` to tell our visitors that they can embed videos:

```
<h3>Add Videos to JazzMeet!</h3>
You can now add videos to JazzMeet using the following code:
<tt>
<video>YouTube video ID</video>
</tt>

Videos from Google Video can be added with the following code:
<tt>
<video type="googlevideo">Google video ID</video>
</tt>
For more information, see [[Help:Adding videos to JazzMeet]].
```

This changes the message in the edit interface of our JazzMeet wiki to:

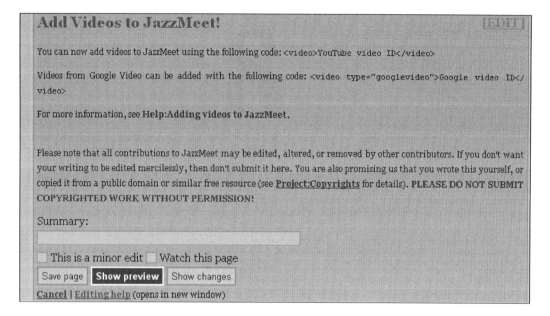

Social Bookmarking

Social bookmarking allows people to "bookmark", or make a note of, the websites they like or find useful, and share these bookmarks with other social bookmarkers while surfing the Internet.

Traditionally, bookmarking was done through the Internet browsing software, such as Internet Explorer, Safari, Firefox, or Opera. With social bookmarking, your bookmarks are not confined to one browser, but are stored online.

The following two options are available for enabling social bookmarking on your website:

- Link to each individual social bookmarking service that you wish to use
- Use a social bookmarking aggregator such as Socializer or AddThis

Even if you do not have links to allow visitors to bookmark your website, many services allow their users to install toolbars in their browser, which allows your website to be added anyway. Adding these links will help to spread your wiki and its new skin very fast.

Individual Social Bookmarking Services

There are huge numbers of social bookmarking services on the Internet, and quite a number of these have become reasonably popular. We will look at some of the more popular bookmarking services such as:

- Mister Wong
- Furl
- Facebook

Your Wiki's Audience

One thing to consider before adding social bookmarking service links to your wiki is your audience. For instance, if your wiki is technology-related, you may find it better to use Digg than Facebook, as Digg is more popular than Facebook for your wiki's intended audience. If your wiki's visitors are primarily from Germany, you may find Mister Wong more useful than Furl, because Mister Wong is more popular with the German users.

There are many other social bookmarking services available, including Del.icio. us (`http://del.icio.us`) and StumbleUpon (`http://stumbleupon.com`), which you can use after asking your wiki's visitors by means of a poll, or following simple experimentation.

Example of Audience

durhamStudent (`http://durhamStudent.co.uk`) is a niche website aimed at students of Durham University in the UK:

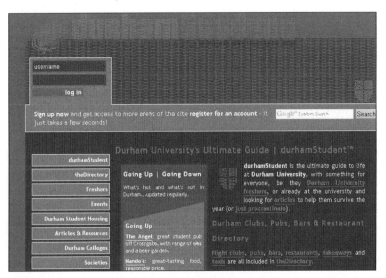

The durhamStudent website uses both the methods of social bookmarking discussed earlier, providing links for eKstreme's Socializer and a link to an individual bookmarking service, Facebook:

Facebook was linked individually here because it is incredibly popular among the students at Durham University (indeed, the Durham network is only open to those with a university email address). Although Facebook's bookmarking service is accessible through Socializer, it is also linked separately as the website's target audience is more likely to use that service than any other.

Mister Wong

Mister Wong, http://www.mister-wong.com, is popular with German and other European users (though not so much in Great Britain), and allows the users to store their bookmarks while maintaining their privacy, with the ability to set bookmarks as "public" or "private".

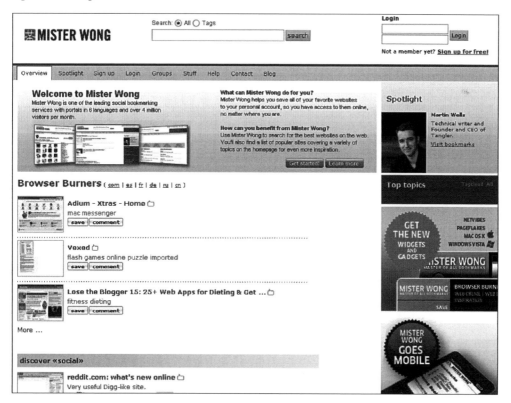

Generally, the social bookmarking services ask for two pieces of information when creating a link from your website to them: the URL (address) of the page or website you want to add, and the title of that page or website, as you wish it to be posted.

Linking to Mister Wong

To link to Mister Wong, create a link where you want your social bookmark to be shown in your MediaWiki template in the following format:

```
http://www.mister-wong.com/index.php?action=addurl&bm_url=www.example.
com &bm_description=Your+Website
```

 Spaces are automatically escaped with a "+" sign by the majority of social bookmarking services. You don't have to worry about properly escaping spaces in the title of your link when linking to bookmarking services.

To use these services with MediaWiki, we will be required to use some PHP that we covered in Chapter 5. In particular, we will need the following:

- The page's title, which we can get with
  ```
  <?php $this->text('pagetitle') ?>
  ```
- The website's address, retrievable with
  ```
  <?php $this->urlencode('serverurl') ?>
  ```

For simplicity, we will assume that our visitors will always want to bookmark JazzMeet's homepage, `http://www.jazzmeet.com`. Thus, the code in our MediaWiki template would appear as follows:

```
<a href= "http://www.mister-wong.com/index.php?action=addurl&bm_
url=www.jazzmeet.com &bm_description=JazzMeet" title="Bookmark
JazzMeet with Mister Wong">Bookmark JazzMeet with Mister Wong</a>
```

What Mister Wong Users See

If a visitor to your wiki decides to bookmark your wiki with Mister Wong, they will be greeted with a screen similar to the following, with fields for the address of the website (URL), title, related keywords ("tags"), and a comment about the website:

They are also given the option to bookmark as either "public", allowing other Mister Wong users to see it, or "private", which restricts the bookmarked website to their account only.

Furl

Furl, `http://www.furl.net`, has functionality that is similar to Mister Wong.

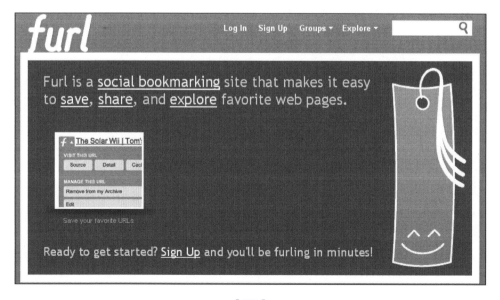

Linking to Furl

Very similar to Mister Wong, you can create a link to bookmark a particular page in MediaWiki by inserting the following in to your skin template:

```
<a href= "http://www.furl.net/storeIt.jsp?t=JazzMeet&u=www.jazzmeet.
com" title="Bookmark JazzMeet with Furl">Bookmark JazzMeet with Furl</
a>
```

What Furl Users See

Furl has the same features as Mister Wong. But the Furl team has added its own twist to social bookmarking, with the added features of being able to add a rating (out of five stars), marking the bookmark as "read" or "unread", and creating "groups" to better organize your bookmarked websites:

This information is provided by the user, so you don't need to specify any more parameters in addition to the page title and your wiki's address.

Facebook

Facebook (`http://facebook.com`) is a very popular social networking site that allows people to share photographs with each other. In 2006, Facebook launched its social bookmarking feature.

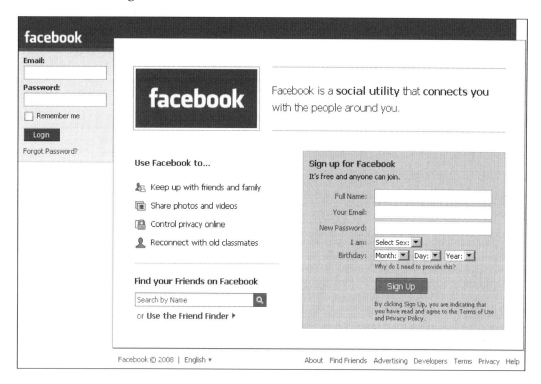

Linking to Facebook

To link to Facebook's social bookmarking service, we can use the following code:

```
<a href= " http://www.facebook.com/sharer.php?u=http://www.jazzmeet.
com" title="Bookmark JazzMeet with Facebook">Bookmark JazzMeet with
Facebook</a>
```

Note that we do not need to specify the page's title, as Facebook will automatically insert this, along with an (optional) image and a brief description of your website.

What Facebook Users See

Facebook's sharing features are a lot more limited than other social bookmarking services. The user is given an option to change the title or the address being bookmarked, and write a short description of the website:

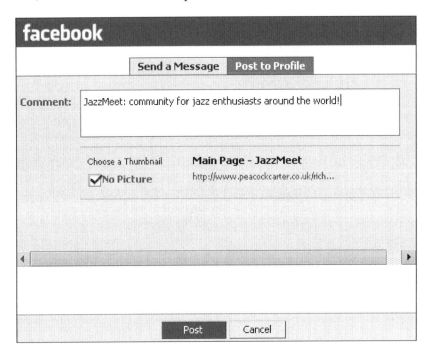

Once posted, the link is visible in the poster's feed:

Social Bookmarking Aggregators

Rather than attempting to put every single social bookmarking site link in your MediaWiki skin template, there is a simpler way. We can use a social bookmark aggregator such as eKstreme's Socializer, or AddThis.

AddThis

AddThis (`http://addthis.com`) is the "number one bookmarking and sharing button".

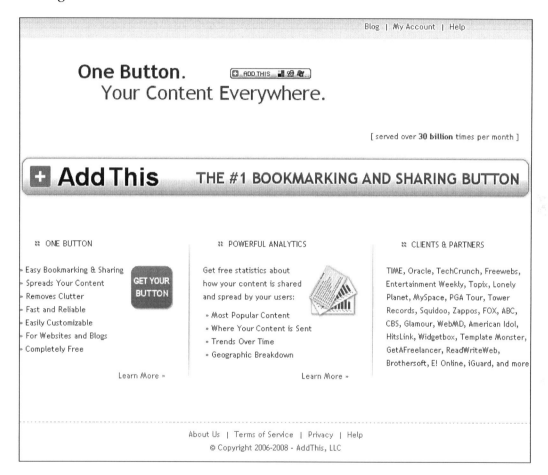

Linking to AddThis

Linking to AddThis is easy as there is a wizard-style, step-by-step guide for creating and customizing your button. AddThis gives you a number of choices as to how it looks and acts for your wiki's visitors. Firstly, it can be used as a single button:

Secondly, a "drop-down" version with JavaScript can be used, which provides an instant access to the more popular bookmarking services:

 You may need to register for an "AddThis" account to gain access to the code that will be required.

Socializer

ekStreme's Socializer (`http://ekstreme.com/socializer`) is another social bookmark service aggregator.

Unlike AddThis, Socializer does not have a drop-down "widget", so to use it you can just link to it as you would do in any other website.

>
>
> **New Windows**
>
> You can create a new browser window by adding `target="_blank"` to the relevant link attribute. You could use this to prevent your wiki's visitors from losing their place on your wiki when they bookmark it. But it may irritate some visitors who are accustomed to opening a new tab in their browser by using the central mouse button.

Linking to Socializer

Linking to Socializer is similar to linking to Mister Wong or Furl's social bookmarking services.

```
<a href= "http://ekstreme.com/socializer/?url=www.jazzmeet.
com&title=JazzMeet" title="Bookmark JazzMeet with Socializer">Bookmark
JazzMeet with Socializer</a>
```

What Socializer Users See

Socializer users are presented with a list of bookmarking services, with a more popular group towards the top of the screen:

Social bookmarking for JazzMeet

As JazzMeet's visitors are likely to be from a wide range of backgrounds, we will use eKstreme's Socializer for JazzMeet's social bookmarking.

Insert the XHTML given earlier in JazzMeet's skin template, below the article's content, aligned to the right:

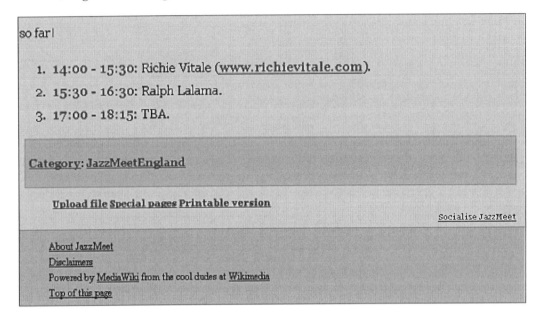

Summary

We have covered embedding links to social networking sites and more interactive elements in your website, including the following:

- Videos from YouTube, Google Video, and other popular video sharing websites
- Twitter feeds
- Social bookmarks

Although adding these more interactive features to your wiki can be a good thing, remember that they should only be used to enhance your wiki, and not as its primary focus. Without useful content, your wiki's visitors will leave your wiki and not add anything to the community that you are trying to create.

9
Deploying Your MediaWiki Skin

In the previous chapters, we have covered the topics that helped us in making our MediaWiki skin ready to deploy across the wiki. You can not use use your new skin on the wiki, but can also share your creation with members of the MediaWiki community. In this chapter, we will cover the following:

- The licensing options you could use with your skin
- Packaging your MediaWiki skin for use by others
- Deploying your skin on your own wiki

Deploying on your Own Wiki

We have briefly covered how to deploy your MediaWiki skin across your wiki in Chapter 2. But even if you used your wiki's new skin as your user account's preferred skin, you can still change the the wiki's settings so that all of your wiki's visitors will be able to use it.

Simply set `$wgDefaultSkin` variable in the `LocalSettings.php` file to the name of your skin. To make the JazzMeet skin as the default skin for your wiki, replace `$wgDefaultSkin = 'monobook'` with `$wgDefaultSkin = 'jazzmeet'`. Remember to upload the file to its original location once you have replaced it.

Packaging Your MediaWiki Skin

If you want to share your MediaWiki skin with the MediaWiki community, you can package it for a general use and post it to Wikimedia in the user styles gallery (`http://meta.wikimedia.org/wiki/Gallery_of_user_styles`).

What Needs to be Included

You will need to include the contents of your skin's directory, including the `main.css` file and any images in it. For the JazzMeet skin, all of these will be in the `skins/jazzmeet/` directory of your wiki's installation directory.

Additionally, you should include the PHP template file associated with your new skin. For JazzMeet, this is located in the `skins/` directory, and is called `JazzMeet.php`.

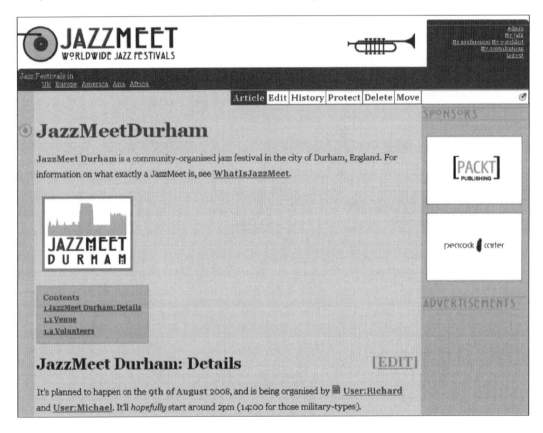

 Do remember to include the print stylesheet, and any changes you have made to it. This is available in `skins/common/`, and is called `commonPrint.css`.

If you made any changes to the `LocalSettings.php` file, you may want to include that in your skin's package, as well. Do not worry about doing this if you have only made changes to the skin name, as we can get help on Wikimedia's website for setting a new skin as the default skin.

It is also better to mention any other files that have been changed, and the elements that have been hidden from the default MediaWiki layout, such as the toolbox or the personal navigation bar. This helps MediaWiki users who may want to use your skin understand how it differs from the traditional MediaWiki skins, and to know whether any changes need to be made to your skin for their use.

README File

It is traditional to include a README.txt file in your wiki skin's package to provide information about yourself, such as your contact name, or for feedback, and bug reports. You can also mention the browsers in which you have tested your MediaWiki skin. (It is useful if you have tested it in the most recent versions, for example, of Internet Explorer and Firefox.) It is also useful to mention the version of MediaWiki that you were using while designing your skin.

Our JazzMeet skin's README file may appear as follows:

```
===========================

JazzMeet Skin, version 1.25

===========================

September 2008.

R.W.E. Carter of Peacock Carter for Packt Publishing
-- England, United Kingdom
-- jazzmeet.wiki@googlemail.com

This work is released under the Creative Commons 'Attribution-Non-
Commercial-No Derivative Works' License.

Please contact me with any bugs you may find, and if you manage to fix
one, I'd be grateful to know about it!

Geekery
=======
Tested in Firefox 2.0, Internet Explorer 6 and 7 and Opera 9.26.

Designed using MediaWiki 1.11.0.

Using This Skin
===============
To use this skin, copy all of the images and the CSS (style) files
(included in the jazzmeet/ directory) to the skins directory of your
MediaWiki installation. Copy the JazzMeet.php file in to the skins
directory too.

All you need to do now is to change the $wgDefaultSkins parameter in
your LocalSettings.php file to jazzmeet, and upload it back to your
server, and you're good to go!
Deviations
```

```
==========
The JazzMeet skin differs from MonoBook, with deviations including:
The left hand column is right-aligned, and designed to hold adverts
The majority of the navigation links have been hidden or removed, as
the skin uses static links in the menu
Some links in the footer are hidden or removed

Known Bugs
==========
- None at present
```

The following information is very useful and can be included in your MediaWiki skin's README file:

- Your name (or alias)

- Your contact details that are useful for others to report bugs or suggest improvements to you

- The date of your skin's release

- The version of MediaWiki with which you used your skin can be found on the `Special:Version` page of your wiki.

- A "changelog", which is a list of any changes that you have made to the skin since releasing it

- Major deviations from the more popular MediaWiki skins

- The browsers with which you have tested your skins

You don't have to provide any of this information, but doing so helps others who may want to use your MediaWiki skin, and providing these details is in the spirit of MediaWiki of collaborating with others.

Formats and Compression

To make the download of your MediaWiki skin faster, you could compress it using a common format such as ZIP (**.zip**) and Tar (**.tar**). This is especially useful if your skin uses large images such as photographic background images.

Tar Compression

The latter of these formats, the UNIX-based "Tar", is used by Wikimedia to package the MediaWiki download, and is usually compressed again using GZIP (`http://www.gzip.org`) to form a **.tar.gz** file:

Version française
Home site

The   home page

- Important security patch
- Introduction
- Sources
- Executables
- Frequently Asked Questions
- Related links

This is because Tar simply concatenates (joins) multiple files together, creating what is known as a "Tarball", which is not compressed.

 You can find a tutorial on using Tars at `http://www.cs.duke.edu/ ~ola/courses/programming/tar.html`.

ZIP Compression

There are many programs to deal with Windows-based ZIP compression, including 7-Zip (`http://www.7-zip.org`), WinZip (`http://www.winzip.com`), and PowerArchiver (`http://www.powerarchiver.com`).

 ZIP in Windows

More recent versions of Windows include the ability to "zip" and "unzip" files – just right-click and select **New | Compressed (zipped) folder**.

Licensing Options

You might have spent considerable time skinning MediaWiki. It is, therefore, important to know your options when releasing your skin for others, and the ways in which you can restrict your skin's use by commercial entities.

Usual Licensing and Copyright

By default, all of the graphics that you have created for your wiki will be in your copyright; they are your intellectual property. In the United Kingdom and other members of the European Union, this lasts until 70 years after your death, thanks to "Directive 2006/116/EC" and the consequent legislation. 70 years holds for the United States too, although there are some cases (for example, anonymous work) where the copyright expires after 95 years.

 If your MediaWiki skin is based on the elements of others' work be aware that, depending on the license they released it under, you may have agreed to release your efforts under the same license.

Creative Commons

Creative Commons (`http://creativecommons.org`) has a range of licenses under which your MediaWiki skin can be released:

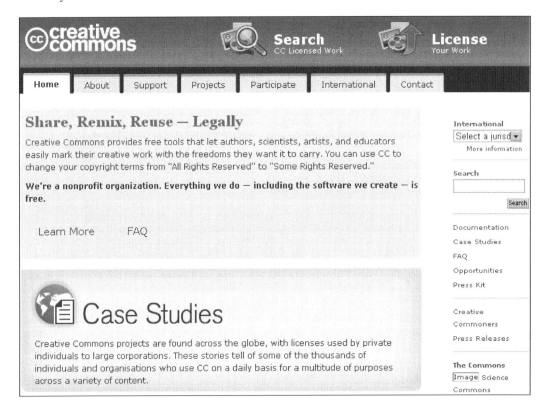

Creative Commons licenses are designed to be less restrictive than traditional copyright. For example, Creative Commons allows for alterations to be made to your MediaWiki skin as long as it is released under the same license.

Parts of Creative Commons License

Creative Commons licenses have the following three parts:

- The Commons deeds
- The legal code
- The digital code

Commons Deeds

The Commons deeds are a summary of the license that uses plain, simple language to describe the basic concepts of the license.

Legal Code

The legal code is the full license that legally binds any users of your MediaWiki skin, should you choose to distribute your skin under the license.

Digital Code

The digital code is the machine-readable version of the license, intended to be used by search engines to help identify the results that have a particular license, and results are without certain restrictions.

Attribution License

With the Creative Commons Attribution license, others are free to modify and distribute your work as long as they acknowledge the original author (s), and provide the subject material to the same license.

The Commons deeds of the Attribution license for people in the UK (England and Wales) will look similar to the following one: (Note the British flag at the top right of the screen.)

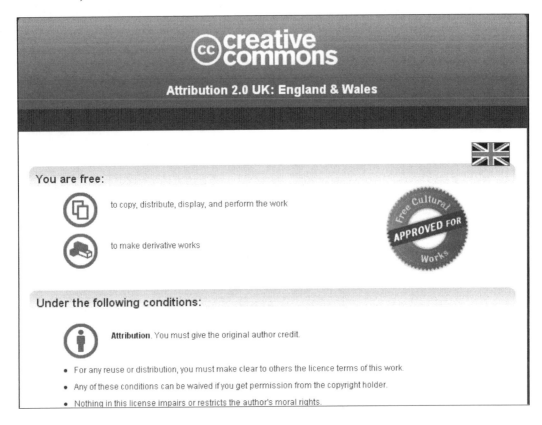

Attribution-Non-Commercial License

The Creative Commons Attribution-Non-Commercial license is similar to the Attribution license, but requires that the work is used for non-commercial purposes only. This license may be ideal for your MediaWiki skin if you want to release it for use by others, as long as they do not benefit from it financially.

England and Wales' Commons deeds for the Creative Commons Attribution-non-Commercial license looks like this:

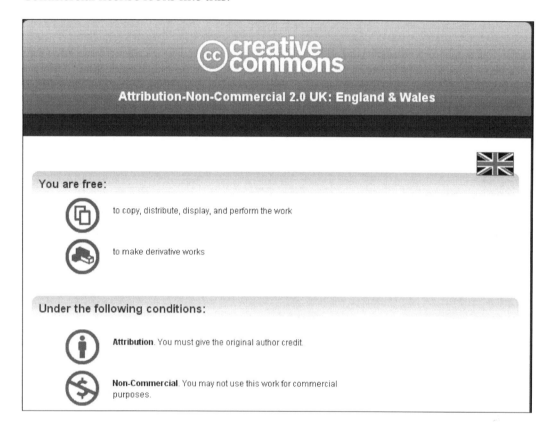

Attribution-Non-Commercial-No Derivative Works License

The Attribution-Non-Commercial-No Derivative Works license follows the Attribution-Non-Commercial license. It allows the use of your wiki's skin, as long as it is not for commercial use, and that the others do not create work based on your MediaWiki skin. The author must be attributed, too.

The Commons deed for this license, applicable to those in England and Wales, shows more restrictions on your skin's use than the previous licenses:

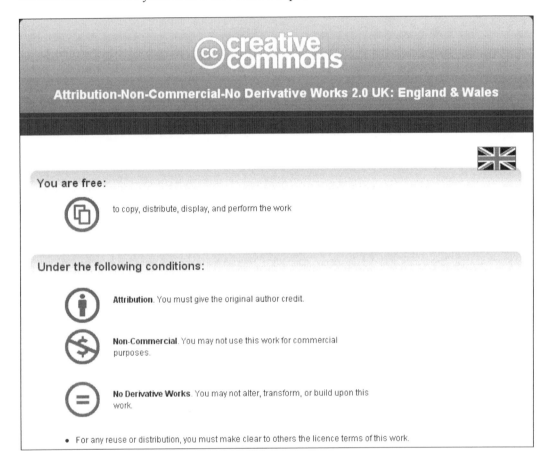

Attribution-Non-Commercial-Share Alike License

The Attribution-Non-Commercial-Share Alike license from the Creative Commons allows your MediaWiki skin to be used and distributed by others, although the original author (you) gets credit for the work, and the work cannot be used for commercial purposes.

The twist with this license is that should anyone build upon or transform your work, they must release their work under the same license, as the Commons deeds shows:

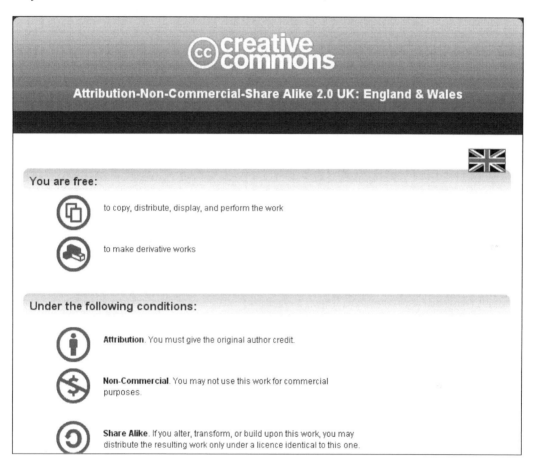

Attribution-No Derivative Works License

Creative Common's Attribution-No Derivative Works license allows others to use your MediaWiki skin, as long as they do not create any work based upon your skin, and credit you as the author of the work:

Attribution-No Derivative Works 2.0 UK: England & Wales

You are free:

to copy, distribute, display, and perform the work

Under the following conditions:

Attribution. You must give the original author credit.

No Derivative Works. You may not alter, transform, or build upon this work.

- For any reuse or distribution, you must make clear to others the licence terms of this work.
- Any of these conditions can be waived if you get permission from the copyright holder.
- Nothing in this license impairs or restricts the author's moral rights.

Attribution-Share Alike 2.0 License

The Attribution-Share Alike license allows derivative works to be made from your MediaWiki skin, as long as you are attributed as its original author and any material based upon your work is released under the same license:

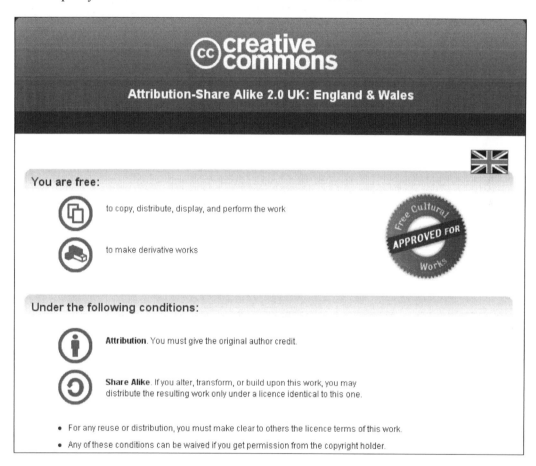

As this England and Wales version of the Commons deed shows, it is approved for "free cultural works" by Freedom Defined (`http://freedomdefined.org`):

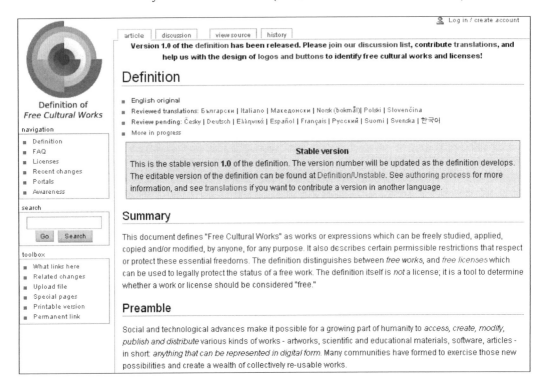

Freedom Defined is working on creating definitions of "free cultural works", and in creating guidelines as to whether a work or a license can be considered "free".

License comparison

Freedom Defined has a matrix of various licenses and their restrictions. It is available at: `http://freedomdefined.org/Licenses`.

Understand the License

Though we have seen a summary of each of the Creative Commons licenses, you should read the full text of the license before licensing your work under it, to prevent misunderstandings in the future.

Waiving the Restrictions

You are free to waive these restrictions to anyone at any time, which is explained towards the bottom of the Commons deeds.

GNU Licenses

The GNU licenses are based upon the licenses written by Richard Stallman for the GNU operating system, and work around the concept of "copyleft" (`http://www.gnu.org/copyleft/`). Copyleft allows everyone, including companies and other profitable organizations, to use and make changes to the materials under the license, so long as they share what they change with the rest of the community.

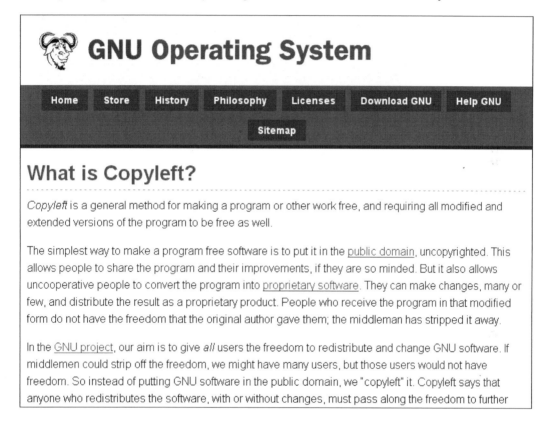

The GNU General Public License (GPL) (`http://www.gnu.org/copyleft/gpl.html`) was written for the use of the institutions and individuals who were not connected with GNU. The GPL would allow others to use your MediaWiki skin so long as any derived work is made available under the same terms.

The GNU Lesser General Public License (LGPL) (`http://www.gnu.org/copyleft/lgpl.html`) is similar to the GPL, but allows the linking of other proprietary or free software or existing work within it. This will prove useful when you have used the work of others in your new MediaWiki skin.

Summary

In this chapter, we have covered deploying your MediaWiki skin and packaging it for the use by others. In particular, we have covered the following:

- Packaging your MediaWiki skin for others to use
- Options for licensing your MediaWiki skin for others to use:
    - Creative Commons
    - The GNU licenses, GPL and LGPL

10
MediaWiki Print Styles

The techniques we have encountered so far for skinning MediaWiki have only applied to the "screen" version of your wiki. In this chapter, we will go through the following:

- The current `commonPrint.css` print stylesheet
- Creating a print stylesheet for your MediaWiki
- Introducing useful CSS elements for the print stylesheet

Viewing the Printable Version of Your Page

The printable version of each page (minus "special" pages such as `Special:Login`) is linked to from each page using links within the "Tools" menu by default, which is identifiable in CSS with `#t-print`. In most modern browsers (such as Internet Explorer 7, Firefox, and Opera 9), if a visitor selects the "print preview" option, the print stylesheet will be used by default.

 Some browsers may add page numbers and the URL of the printed page along with the header and footer of the printed document.

URLs in MediaWiki

The way in which URLs (the addresses of pages) in MediaWiki are displayed depends on the way in which PHP is installed on your wiki's server. If PHP runs as an Apache module, the URLs are seen as `wiki/index.php/Article_Title`. If PHP runs as a CGI (Common Gateway Interface) module, the URLs will be seen as `wiki/index.php?title=Article_Title`.

Print URL

Let us assume that a normal page title in MediaWiki is `wiki/index.php/ Article_Title`, where `wiki/` is the directory of MediaWiki's install on your wiki's server. The printable version of the page is accessible via the URL `wiki/index. php?title=Article_Title&printable=yes`.

The `&printable=yes` parameter added to the URL specifies that the printable version of the page should be displayed. The URL for MediaWiki uses the friendly URL structure. For example, `wiki/Article_Title` uses the same printable URL `wiki/index.php?title=Article_Title&printable=yes`.

Wiki Markup

You can insert wiki markup into pages, to insert a link in the printable version of pages on your wiki:

```
{{SERVER}}{{localurl:{{PAGENAME}}|printable=yes}}
```

Escape your HTML

To maintain the validity of the XHTML in your wiki, remember that when inserting an ampersand ("&") in to your skin's MediaWiki template, you will need to "escape" it using the `&amp;` character entity. This is particularly important in URLs, where `link. html?d=content&e=more-content` should be `link.html?d=conte nt&amp;e=more-content`.

What's Already Done for Us: commonPrint.css

The default print stylesheet for MediaWiki is linked to within the `<head>` element of your wiki's template file. It is called `commonPrint.css`, and is stored in the `skins/ common/` directory of your MediaWiki installation.

You can add additional styling to this file to accommodate your new skin, although changing the CSS in this file will cause the print styling for other MediaWiki skins to change too.

Backup commonPrint.css **before you alter it.**

Creating a backup copy of the commonPrint.css file is a good idea as it could be useful for future reference. If you decide to remove your skin, you can simply replace the previous version of the file to keep the CSS file's size small.

The body of the document is styled to have a white background and black text to make printed copies of the content easier to read:

```
body {
background: White;
color: Black;
margin: 0;
padding: 0;
}
```

A Separate Print Stylesheet

If you are planning to alter other skins' print styling, you can create a new print stylesheet for your new skin. Just remember to link to it in your template's header:

```
<style type="text/css" title="Default page style" media="print">
<!--@import "skins/jazzmeet/print.css";-->
</style>
```

Commenting out the stylesheet's import

By commenting out the @import statement, you can prevent older Internet browsers from becoming perplexed. So it is a good practice to get into.

External Links

A rather nice feature of MediaWiki's print styling is that where an external link is given, it will append the link text with the absolute URL of the external page that is linked to. This is shown in the following example (contrasted with an internal link) in browsers other than Internet Explorer:

- Internal link
- External link (http://www.peacockcarter.com/)

This is done by the following CSS in the `commonPrint.css` file:

```
#content a.external.text:after, #content a.external.autonumber:after {
/* Expand URLs for printing */
content: " (" attr(href) ") ";
}
```

Page Content

The print stylesheet sets the width of the content on your wiki to "100" percent of the page, so that there is no unnecessary white space on a visitor's printed page. It also redefines colors, padding, and margins of the main content areas to values suitable for printing:

```
#globalWrapper {
width: 100% !important;
min-width: 0 !important;
}
#content {
background : white;
color : black;
}
#column-content {
margin: 0 !important;
}
#column-content #content {
padding: 1em;
margin: 0 !important;
}
```

Lists are also restyled to have square bullet points when printed:

```
ul {
list-style-type: square;
}
```

Serif or non-serif fonts

Serif fonts (for example, "Times", "Times New Roman", and "Georgia") are supposedly easier to read on paper than sans-serif fonts more commonly used on screen (those such as "Arial", "Verdana", and "Helvetica"). You may want to consider redefining your wiki's print stylesheet to use serif fonts for its print version.

Site Notice

The #siteNotice div contains the wiki-wide message as defined on the MediaWiki: Sitenotice page:

This is a site notice - JazzMeetDurham

By default, MediaWiki's commonPrint.css file hides this element from printing:

```
#siteNotice {
display: none;
}
```

Table of Contents

By default, the table of contents in MediaWiki (#toc) is shown in the print version, and margins surrounding the various levels of the table of contents' hierarchy are reset to sensible values:

```
#toc {
border:1px solid #aaaaaa;
background-color:#f9f9f9;
padding:5px;
}
.tocindent {
margin-left: 2em;
}
.tocline {
margin-bottom: 0px;
}
```

Some more CSS is relevant to the table of contents which again resets indents:

```
.tocindent p {
margin: 0 0 0 0 ! important;
}
```

Images

Some restyling of images in the page is undertaken, including re-coloring borders and assigning margins, and also in ensuring that images flow within the document for the purpose of printing:

```
div.floatright {
float: right;
clear: right;
margin: 0;
position:relative;
border: 0.5em solid White;
border-width: 0.5em 0 0.8em 1.4em;
}
div.floatright p {
font-style: italic;
}
div.floatleft {
float: left;
margin: 0.3em 0.5em 0.5em 0;
position:relative;
border: 0.5em solid White;
border-width: 0.5em 1.4em 0.8em 0;
}
div.floatleft p {
font-style: italic;
}
```

Thumbnail Images

As with full images, the thumbnail images in your wiki page are also restyled to ensure that they are displayed properly on paper. Notably, the "magnify" icon is hidden:

```
div.thumb {
margin-bottom: 0.5em;
border-style: solid; border-color: White;
width: auto;
overflow: hidden;
}
div.thumb div {
border:1px solid #cccccc;
padding: 3px !important;
background-color:#f9f9f9;
font-size: 94%;
text-align: center;
}
div.thumb div a img {
```

```
border:1px solid #cccccc;
}
div.thumb div div.thumbcaption {
border: none;
padding: 0.3em 0 0.1em 0;
}
div.magnify {
display: none;
}
div.tright {
float: right;
clear: right;
border-width: 0.5em 0 0.8em 1.4em;
}
div.tleft {
float: left;
margin-right:0.5em;
border-width: 0.5em 1.4em 0.8em 0;
}
img.thumbborder {
border: 1px solid #dddddd;
}
```

Diff - document difference pages

MediaWiki's default print style also caters to the "diff" pages that display the difference between two versions of the same page within the wiki. As with the rest of print styling, the tables used in "diff" pages are styled with black as the text color and white as the background color, while subtly highlighting the areas that have changed with a light grey background (#CCFFCC, #FFFFAA):

```
table.diff {
background:white;
}
td.diff-otitle {
background:#ffffff;
}
td.diff-ntitle {
background:#ffffff;
}
td.diff-addedline {
background:#ccffcc;
font-size: smaller;
border: solid 2px black;
}
td.diff-deletedline {
background:#ffffaa;
font-size: smaller;
border: dotted 2px black;
```

```
}
td.diff-context {
background:#eeeeee;
font-size: smaller;
}
.diffchange {
color: silver;
font-weight: bold;
text-decoration: underline;
}
```

Links

Some links are also restyled for the printable version of your wiki pages. The internal links in your wiki are de-styled, whereas the external links, and links to pages on your wiki that have not yet been created:

```
a, a.external, a.new, a.stub {
color: black ! important;
text-decoration: none ! important;
}
a, a.external, a.new, a.stub {
color: inherit ! important;
text-decoration: inherit ! important;
}
```

 The second statement is for non-Internet Explorer browsers which understand the inherit statement.

Footer and Miscellaneous Elements

The print stylesheet explicitly hides a number of elements in the page for printing, including a number of links contained within list items in the footer and the "powered by MediaWiki" badge. It also includes navigation surrounding the primary content area, `#column-one`:

```
.noprint, div#jump-to-nav, div.top, div#column-one, #colophon,
.editsection, .toctoggle, .tochidden, div#f-poweredbyico, div#f-
copyrightico, li#viewcount, li#about, li#disclaimer, li#privacy {
display: none;
}
```

What Remains to be Styled

JazzMeet's on-line styling is also reasonable for a printable version of the wiki, but we can still make some modifications to it.

JazzMeetDurham

(Redirected from **Content**)

JazzMeet Durham is a community-organised jazz festival in the city of Durham, England. For information on what exactly a JazzMeet is, see **WhatIsJazzMeet**.

Contents   [HIDE]

JazzMeet Durham: Details

It's planned to happen on the 9th of August 2008, and is being organised by **User:Richard** and **User:Michael**. It'll *hopefully* start around 2pm (14:00 for those military-types).

Venue

The venue is **Collingwood College (http://www.dur.ac.uk/collingwood)** (Durham University (http://www.dur.ac.uk)), which has a maximum capacity of 150.

Volunteers

As with every JazzMeet event, these people have kindly volunteered to donate the following goodies at JazzMeet Durham:

An example image

- T-shirts: **User:David** of **Packt (http://www.packtpub.com)**.
- Door woman (14:00 - 18:30): **User:DS**.
- Ticket printing + design: **User:Richard** of **Peacock, Carter & Associates (http://www.peacockcarter.co.uk)**.

Want to help?

Great! Add your name below.

Add Your Name Here

Food	User:Michael	Sarah
Drink	Danielle	User:Richard
Tickets (on the door)	User:David	User:Richard

MORE DETAILS

Contact **User:Richard** for more details.

The Bands

The most important part of JazzMeet events is the **music**, and we've got some great artists lined up so far!

1. 14:00 - 15:30: Richie Vitale (**www.richievitale.com (http://www.richievitale.com)**).
2. 15:30 - 16:30: Ralph Lalama.
3. 17:00 - 18:15: TBA.

Category: **JazzMeetEngland**

The printable version of our wiki's pages looks good at the moment, but we can make them a little easier to read when we print them by removing the colors in tables and table of contents.

Content

Any text surrounded with `<strong>` or `<b>` tags in JazzMeet still appear red, so we need to reset this for the printable version of our wiki:

```
#globalWrapper strong, #globalWrapper b {
color: #000000 !important;
}
```

Table of Contents

After styling the table of contents for JazzMeet, the print version's styling for the table of contents is overwritten:

We can use `!important` statements in the existing CSS to ensure that the colors are overwritten. Just in case, we will also set the color of the content in the table of contents to black:

```
#toc {
border:1px solid #aaaaaa !important;
background-color:#f9f9f9 !important;
color: #000000 !important;
padding:5px;
}
```

The `<h2>` level heading that contains the table of contents' title still appears red, so we need to reset this to black, too:

```
#toc h2 {
color: #000000 !important;
}
```

Categories

The category box still has its color from JazzMeet's main stylesheet:

Because users printing the pages will not be able to click the category links on your wiki's pages, we can hide these links.

```
#catlinks {
display: none !important;
}
```

Tables of Data

Tables of data in the printable version of the JazzMeet skin are still partially colored:

Food	User:Michael	Sarah
Drink	Danielle	User:Richard
Tickets (on the door)	User:David	User:Richard

We will simply reset the colors in table header cells (`<th>`). Refer to the following code:

```
table th {
background: #DDDDDD !important;
color: #000000 !important;
}
```

This leaves a more print-friendly table in our printable page, but the border's color around the normal table cells (`<td>`) is still beige, which can be changed to gray using the following code:

```
table td {
border-color: #DDDDDD !important;
}
```

Food	User:Michael	Sarah
Drink	Danielle	User:Richard
Tickets (on the door)	User:David	User:Richard

Footer

You can add the class `.noprint` to elements in your MediaWiki template to render them invisible in the printable version of the page. We can apply this to the two list items in the footer that will not be required on paper. Refer to the following code:

```
.f-poweredby, .f-top {
display: none;
}
```

In fact, we can hide the entire footer in the JazzMeet skin, since our "printfooter" is contained outside the following:

```
#footer {
display: none !important;
}
```

Printfooter

`.printfooter` contains a reference to your wiki, that is, the location where your visitor found the information he or she is printing. So it is a good idea to provide a reference as to where the information came from:

```
.printfooter {
font-size: 75%;
display: block;
margin-left: 10px;
visibility: visible;
}
```

New Message Notification

As it stands, the print stylesheet still shows the "new message" notification window:

Because there is no link on a paper that a user can click on, this will not be of any use to your wiki's visitors to check their messages. So we can hide the `.usermessage` div with some simple CSS. Refer to the following code:

```
.usermessage {
display: none !important
}
```

Summary

In this chapter, we covered the following:

- The existing print stylesheet, `commonPrint.css`
- Building on the existing print stylesheet provided with MediaWiki

This chapter helps us in removing all unnecessary elements from the general wiki's skin, and using colors with good contrast. It also explained how to minimize the amount of ink used by your visitors to print each page.

A

Troubleshooting Browser Issues with MediaWiki

Our new skin for the JazzMeet wiki appears to function correctly in the following browsers: Internet Explorer 7, Firefox 2, and Opera 9. In this appendix, we will look at the following:

- The modes of interpretation that browsers apply to CSS: Standards mode and Quirks mode
- Conditional comments for Internet Explorer
- Quick fixes to common quirks in Internet Explorer
- Fixes for bugs in other browsers, such as Opera and Firefox

Browser Modes

Internet Explorer and other Internet browsers have two modes when it comes to interpreting your CSS: Standards mode and Quirks mode.

- Quirks mode helps browsers to display websites written in older HTML as they would have been displayed when they were written. If they were displayed within Standards mode, these (probably table-based) designs would break.
- Standards mode is used to interpret websites that provide a doctype (even if the document itself does not actually validate to the provided doctype).

Standards Mode

The use of a doctype, such as the following one, triggers Standards mode in most (if not all) modern browsers:

```
<!DOCTYPE html PUBLIC "-//W3C//DTD XHTML 1.0 Strict//EN" "http://www.
w3.org/TR/xhtml1/DTD/xhtml1-strict.dtd">
```

Quirks Mode

Quirks mode is used by browsers for websites that do not present a doctype at the top of the document.

 For more information on Quirks mode, Wikipedia has an excellent article: http://en.wikipedia.org/wiki/Quirks_mode

Most errors displayed in webpages can be fixed with the application of the correct doctype. It is often worth experimenting with the various doctypes before attempting anything drastic to fix a problem.

Conditional Comments

Because the great majority of web designers use browsers that are more Standards-compliant than Internet Explorer - for example, Firefox, Opera, and Safari — "bugs" tend to appear in some pages when the pages are viewed in Internet Explorer, rather than Firefox.

Conditional comments allow us to serve different stylesheets not only for Internet Explorer, but even targeted to individual version of Internet Explorer.

A conditional comment will be read as a traditional comment in browsers other than Internet Explorer, that is, its contents will be ignored. But Internet Explorer will recognize the syntax of the conditional comments and apply or display whatever is shown within the comment, should the condition apply to the version of Internet Explorer currently interpreting the webpage.

Versionless Conditional Comments in Internet Explorer

If you wish to supply a stylesheet or other content to the visitors of your wiki using Internet Explorer, simply nest it within the following conditional comment syntax:

```
<!--[if IE]>
This will appear in Internet Explorer, but no other browsers.
<![endif]-->
```

For example, if we want to promote the Opera Internet browser (`http://www.opera.com`) to JazzMeet's visitors using Internet Explorer, we could insert the following conditional comment in a suitable place in our MediaWiki skin template:

```
<!--[if IE]>
<div id="use-opera">
Welcome to <strong>JazzMeet</strong>! Have you considered using
another browser such as <a href="http://www.opera.com" title="Opera
browser">Opera</a>?
</div>
<![endif]-->
```

We can apply some styling to the `#use-opera` ID in JazzMeet's CSS to lessen its focus:

```
#use-opera {
background: #E6E4D8;
border-bottom: 2px #8C1425 solid;
color: #38230C;
font-size: 90%;
padding: 10px;
}
#use-opera a {
color: #8C1425;
}
```

Visitors to JazzMeet will now be met with a view similar to the following one for visitors who visit the wiki in Internet Explorer:

Welcome to **JazzMeet**! Have you considered using another browser such as <u>Opera</u>?

JazzMeetDurham

JazzMeet Durham is a community-organised jazz festival in the city of Durham, England. For information on what exactly a JazzMeet is, see **WhatIsJazzMeet**.

In a browser such as Firefox or Opera, we don't see the message:

JazzMeetDurham

JazzMeet Durham is a community-organised jazz festival in the city of Durham, England. For information on what exactly a JazzMeet is, see **WhatIsJazzMeet**.

Version-Based Conditional Comments in Internet Explorer

We are able to focus on specific versions of Internet Explorer in the following three ways:

- `lt` (less than): If the visitor is using a version of Internet Explorer less than the given value, a message is displayed to your wiki's visitors, for example `<!--[lt IE 6]>This is version of IE is less than 6<![endif]-->`.

- `gte` (greater than or equal to): If the visitor is using a version of Internet Explorer greater than or equal to the given value, a message is displayed to your wiki's visitors for example `<!--[gte IE 7]>This version of IE is 7 or greater<![endif]-->`

- Lastly, you can specify a particular version of Internet Explorer, for example `<!--[IE 5]>This version of IE is 5.<![endif]-->`.

In Chapter 8, we added the ability for our users to add videos from video sharing websites, such as Google Video and YouTube, to the editable section of JazzMeet with the addition of the VideoFlash extension for MediaWiki.

We may want to inform visitors who are using versions of Internet Explorer of less than five to upgrade their browsers to be able to view these videos that we can view with the addition of a conditional comment:

```
<!--[lt IE 5]>
<div id="upgrade-browser">
In order to view videos and other media in the <strong>JazzMeet</
strong> website, we suggest you <a href="http://www.microsoft.
com/windows/downloads/ie/getitnow.mspx" title="Upgrade your
browser">upgrade your version of Internet Explorer</a>.
</div>
<![endif]-->
```

We can apply the same styling as our earlier conditional message:

```
#use-opera,
#upgrade-browser {
background: #E6E4D8;
border-bottom: 2px #8C1425 solid;
color: #38230C;
font-size: 90%;
padding: 10px;
}
#use-opera a,
#upgrade-browser a {
color: #8C1425;
}
```

This presents the following message in versions 4 or less in Internet Explorer:

In order to view videos and other media in the **JazzMeet** website, we suggest you upgrade your version of Internet Explorer.

JazzMeetDurham

JazzMeet Durham is a community-organised jazz festival in the city of Durham, England. For information on what exactly a JazzMeet is, see **WhatIsJazzMeet**.

Stylesheets and Conditional Comments

Another use for these conditional comments is to supply additional stylesheets to Internet Explorer in order to fix discrepancies in the design. Firstly, we will look at some of the major problems that affect each version of Internet Explorer, and then apply fixes for these to our new skin for the JazzMeet wiki.

Conditional Stylesheets

By adding a conditional comment to the `<head>` section of our MediaWiki skin template, we can supply another stylesheet to make some changes to the design for a specific version of Internet Explorer. The following example shows how to link to a stylesheet targeting only Internet Explorer 5:

```
<head>
<!-- other head elements -->
<!--[IE 5]>
<style type="text/css" title="IE5-fixes" media="screen">
<!--@import "skins/jazzmeet/ie5fixes.css";-->
</style>
<![endif]-->
</head>
```

Some older versions of Internet Explorer may still be popular among some of your wiki's visitors, and it may be worth making sure your design is compatible with these.

Internet Explorer 5 Bugs

There are a number of bugs in Internet Explorer 5 that are easily fixed once you know how to do so:

- Background images (such as those used in external links in MediaWiki) do not show.
- The font size of Internet Explorer 5 and 5.5 is offset compared to other browsers.

Background Image Bug

JazzMeet's CSS style links to pages on the wiki that have not been created yet, as follows:

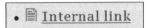

Because Internet Explorer 5 does not render these nicely, we will need to remove these background images. We can create a new stylesheet, `ie5fixes.css`, in the `skins/` directory of our MediaWiki installation, and link to it in the `<head>` of our MediaWiki skin as demonstrated above.

We can then add CSS to overwrite previous styling associated with the "new article" link styling:

```
a.new {
background: none;
padding: 0;
}
```

This removes the background image and the padding given for external links in the previous CSS for JazzMeet's skin:

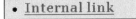

Font-Sizing Bug

Internet Explorer 5 and Internet Explorer 5.5 do not interpret the font-size you set as other browsers do. You can correct this by adding the following CSS to the `ie5fixes.css` file:

```
body {
font-size: xx-small
}
```

This simply tells Internet Explorer 5 to resize the text to a smaller size than other browsers, making the size of text appear consistent across the browsers.

Cursor Hand bug

Another noticeable bug in Internet Explorer 5.5 is that the "pointer" cursor does not appear when you hover over the logo. This can be addressed by the following CSS fix from MonoBook's skin:

```
#p-logo a,
#p-logo a:hover {
    cursor: pointer;
}
```

Internet Explorer 6 Bugs

Some of the common bugs in Internet Explorer 6 that we will fix are as follows:

- The "double-margin" problem
- Inline list items' contents are only partially displayed

Double-Margin Bug

The double-margin bug occurs in Internet Explorer when a floated element, such as a `div`, is given a margin on the side where it is floated.

For example, assume that your MediaWiki skin contains the following HTML:

```
<div id="div-one">
    <div id="div-two">
Div two.
    </div>
</div>
```

The highlighted CSS causes some problem in Internet Explorer:

```
#div-one {
background: #222;
height: 75px;
}
#div-two {
    background: #9C0;
height: 50px;
float: left;
margin-left: 10px
width: 300px;
}
```

Although the colors are just there to show where the two divs are positioned, the float and margin cause problems. In Opera, Firefox, and Safari, this is displayed perfectly:

In Internet Explorer 6, the margin alongside the left of the smaller (green) box is doubled:

Luckily, the fix for this bug is simple. Just add display: inline to the inner div:

```
#div-two {
background: #9C0;
height: 50px;
display: inline;
float: left;
margin-left: 10px
width: 300px;
}
```

The inner container is now displayed as follows in Opera, Firefox, and Safari:

Inline List Items Partially Displayed

Inline lists not being displayed properly is a common problem in Internet Explorer. To demonstrate the problem, we can create an unordered list of hyperlinks:

```
<ul id="test">
<li><a href="#" title="Link title">Link</a></li>
<li><a href="#" title="Link title">Link</a></li>
<li><a href="#" title="Link title">Link</a></li>
</ul>
```

We can now style these to display inline with CSS. Because such styling is usually used to style a list of links as a menu within the webpage, we will add some padding to the list item link:

```
ul#test {
list-style-type: none;
}
```

```
#test li {
display: inline;
}
#test li a {
background: #8C1425;
color: #FFF
padding: 10px;
}
```

In the earlier versions of Internet Explorer, this does not display as we intended:

Firefox, Opera, Safari, and Internet Explorer 7 display it as intended:

To remedy the bug, we can apply `position: relative` to links within the list items:

```
#test li a {
background: #8C1425;
color: #FFF
padding: 10px;
position: relative;
}
```

Internet Explorer now displays the links as the other browsers do, and without the use of a conditional comment to apply additional style to the elements in Internet Explorer:

Bugs in Other Browsers

Unlike Internet Explorer, there is no standard way of determining a browser or its version in HTML alone. To target separate stylesheets at visitors to your wiki using these browsers, the easiest way is probably through the use of JavaScript, as described by Quirks Mode: http://www.quirksmode.org/js/detect.html

Firefox Bugs

Bugs in Firefox are less common than in Internet Explorer, but there are some things that may be useful to fix, including empty divs.

Empty Divs Not Clearing

Some versions of Firefox will not properly interpret an empty `div` that has the `clear: both` CSS attribute assigned to it. To fix this, simply give some padding to the `div` as follows: `padding-top: .01em`

Testing your Design in Multiple Browsers

It is not easy to spot flaws in your design as, even if you have many browsers installed on your computer, you will almost certainly not have access to every browser on every platform.

You can use services such as BrowserCam (`http://www.browsercam.com`) to view your MediaWiki skin's design in multiple browsers without needing access to different operating systems:

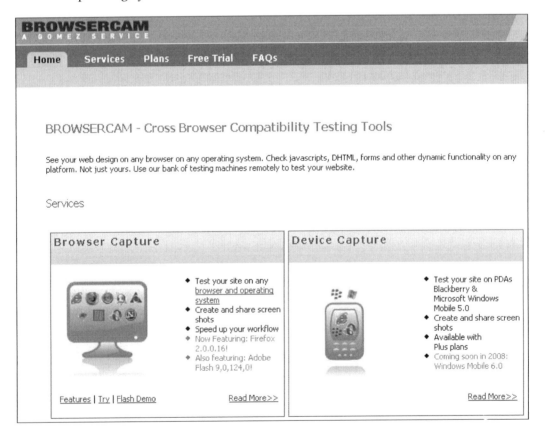

Although BrowserCam is not a free service, you can try it for a limited period with a free trial.

BrowserCam also allows you to see the design as it would be displayed on different devices, including Blackberry handheld devices and other PDAs (personal digital assistants).

Cheaper Alternatives for Testing

If you are redesigning an existing wiki, a cheaper alternative could be to ask a smaller portion of your wiki's community to test a new design before you release it to your live website. Alternatively, you can ask friends and family to test the design on as many different computers and browsers as possible.

Summary

In this appendix, we have covered the following:

- The Standards and Quirks modes in browsers
- How and why the standards and quirks modes are triggered
- Conditional comments in Internet Explorer
- Common browser bugs and their fixes
- Testing your wiki's skin in multiple browsers with services such as BrowserCam

Index

R

recent changes page
  styling 42
redirect pages
  styling 40
registration page
  styling 50, 51

S

search box
  #p-search, styling 69, 70
search results page
  styling 42
serverurl 106
skin
  article content, styling 26
  content body 26
  making, as default skin 25, 26
  making, as wiki's default skin 25
  using 25
skinning, MediaWiki
  features, adding 19
  features, removing 19
  JazzMeet 19, 21
  reasons 18
  usability, improving 19
  widgets, adding 19
  widgets, removing 19
  wiki, distinguishing 18
  wiki, integrating 18
skinning process, MediaWiki
  audience 22
  purpose 21
skinnname 107
social bookmarking
  about 169
  aggregators 176
  enabling, options 169
  facebook 175
  furl 173
  Mister Wong 171
  services 170
  wiki's audience 170
  wiki's audience, example 170, 171
social bookmarking aggregators
  about 176

AddThis 177
ekStreme's Socializer 178, 179
JazzMeet 180
standards mode, browser
  using 211
stylename 107
stylepath 107
styleversion 107

T

Tablecloth, JavaScript
  about 155
  customizing 156
  installing 155
  styles, removing 156
  Tablecloth CSS, adding 155
  tables, highlighting 156
talk pages
  image detail pages, styling 41
  new message, notifying 40
  redirect pages, styling 40
  usermessage used 40
template
  #globalWrapper, inserting 93, 94
  #globalWrapper, styling 94, 95
  content, ordering 92
  content body, changing 97, 98
  content column 95
  creating 90
  elements, ordering 90
  end of file 99
  footer 98
  header 93
  MediaWiki default names, using 90
  order, adopting 91, 92
  resulting pages 99
  two-column layout, creating 92
templates
  blocks, moving around 93
ThickBox, JavaScript
  about 140
  features 141
  images maps 141
  uses 140
toolbox
  #p-tb, styling 66-69

Thank you for buying
MediaWiki Skins Design

Packt Open Source Project Royalties

When we sell a book written on an Open Source project, we pay a royalty directly to that project. Therefore by purchasing MediaWiki Skins Design, Packt will have given some of the money received to the Mdiawiki project.

In the long term, we see ourselves and you—customers and readers of our books—as part of the Open Source ecosystem, providing sustainable revenue for the projects we publish on. Our aim at Packt is to establish publishing royalties as an essential part of the service and support a business model that sustains Open Source.

If you're working with an Open Source project that you would like us to publish on, and subsequently pay royalties to, please get in touch with us.

Writing for Packt

We welcome all inquiries from people who are interested in authoring. Book proposals should be sent to authors@packtpub.com. If your book idea is still at an early stage and you would like to discuss it first before writing a formal book proposal, contact us; one of our commissioning editors will get in touch with you.

We're not just looking for published authors; if you have strong technical skills but no writing experience, our experienced editors can help you develop a writing career, or simply get some additional reward for your expertise.

About Packt Publishing

Packt, pronounced 'packed', published its first book "Mastering phpMyAdmin for Effective MySQL Management" in April 2004 and subsequently continued to specialize in publishing highly focused books on specific technologies and solutions.

Our books and publications share the experiences of your fellow IT professionals in adapting and customizing today's systems, applications, and frameworks. Our solution-based books give you the knowledge and power to customize the software and technologies you're using to get the job done. Packt books are more specific and less general than the IT books you have seen in the past. Our unique business model allows us to bring you more focused information, giving you more of what you need to know, and less of what you don't.

Packt is a modern, yet unique publishing company, which focuses on producing quality, cutting-edge books for communities of developers, administrators, and newbies alike. For more information, please visit our website: www.PacktPub.com.

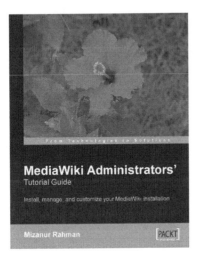

MediaWiki Administrators' Tutorial Guide

ISBN: 978-1-904811-59-6   Paperback: 284 pages

Install, manage, and customize your MediaWiki installation 6

1. Get your MediaWiki site up fast

2. Manage users, special pages, and more

3. Customize and extend your MediaWiki site

4. Create new, attractive MediaWiki themes

Joomla! Template Design

ISBN: 978-1-847191-44-1   Paperback: 250 pages

A complete guide for web designers to all aspects of designing unique website templates for the free Joomla! 1.0.8 PHP Content Management System

1. Create Joomla! Templates for your sites

2. Debug, validate, and package your templates

3. Tips for tweaking existing templates

Please check **www.PacktPub.com** for information on our titles

WordPress Theme Design

ISBN: 978-1-847193-09-4   Paperback: 268 pages

A complete guide to creating professional
WordPress themes

1. Take control of the look and feel of your
   WordPress site

2. Simple, clear tutorial to creating Unique and
   Beautiful themes

3. Expert guidance with practical step-by-step
   instructions for theme design

4. Design tips, tricks, and troubleshooting ide

DotNetNuke Skinning Tutorial

ISBN: 978-1-847192-78-3   Paperback: 144 pages

A simple, clear, step-by-tutorial to creating
DotNetNuke skins to put you in control of the look
and feel of your DotNetNuke website

1. Take control of the look and feel of your
   DotNetNuke website

2. Simple, clear, tutorial to creating DotNetNuke
   skins

3. Practical step-by-step guidance

4. No knowledge of DotNetNuke skinning
   required

Please check **www.PacktPub.com** for information on our titles

Printed in Great Britain by
Amazon.co.uk, Ltd.,
Marston Gate.